Sustainable Investment Policy Perspectives of the East African Community

OECD
BETTER POLICIES FOR BETTER LIVES

This document, as well as any data and map included herein, are without prejudice to the status of or sovereignty over any territory, to the delimitation of international frontiers and boundaries and to the name of any territory, city or area.

Please cite this publication as:
OECD (2024), *Sustainable Investment Policy Perspectives of the East African Community*, OECD Publishing, Paris, https://doi.org/10.1787/169f3378-en.

ISBN 978-92-64-40880-7 (print)
ISBN 978-92-64-45933-5 (PDF)
ISBN 978-92-64-84167-3 (HTML)
ISBN 978-92-64-90299-2 (epub)

Photo credits: Cover © Irfan Quader/GettyImages.

Corrigenda to OECD publications may be found at: https://www.oecd.org/en/publications/support/corrigenda.html.

Foreword

This report introduces OECD tools and analysis to the East African Community (EAC). It is designed as a baseline diagnostic to explore ways to support investment climate reforms in the EAC while providing a greater focus on how to improve sustainable outcomes from investment. The report is also intended to provide insights to the EAC on the preparation of the EAC Investment Strategy, building on the existing EAC Investment Policy (2019). It also aims to support the revision of the EAC Model Investment Code (2006), which the EAC is currently undertaking to align it with the African Continental Free Trade Agreement (AfCFTA), and to provide an analysis of the EAC Model Investment Treaty (2016).

The report starts with an analysis of the impact of foreign direct investment (FDI) on selected areas of sustainable development in EAC Partner States based on the OECD FDI Qualities Indicators. The policy areas covered in this study include the legal framework for investment, including aspects related to protection and non-discrimination of investment, measures to promote and facilitate investment, the use and design of investment incentives, and the promotion of responsible business conduct. The selection of areas builds on the OECD Policy Framework for Investment (PFI) and highlights essential elements of a conducive investment climate, which promotes not only FDI but also sustainable development. The aim is not to provide a ready-made reform agenda for Partner States in the region but rather to explore policy areas that influence investment and its impact. It provides a solid basis for developing a long-term programme of collaboration with the EAC.

Under the overall guidance of Stephen Thomsen, Deputy Head of the Investment Division, the report has been prepared by a team led by Alexandre de Crombrugghe, which included Katharina Böhm, Taufeeq Khan Marcos, Fernando Mistura, Yasmina Najem, Zoé Ryan and Ana Laura Sobalbarro Herrera, from the OECD Investment Division, and Sebastian Weber from the OECD Centre for Responsible Business Conduct. It benefitted from inputs and comments from Fares Al-Hussami, Kiara Blome, Marie Bouchard, Laura Kuusela and Juan Felipe Rodrigo. The report benefitted from editorial assistance and was prepared for publication by Meral Gedik and Lucinda Pearson. The report was prepared in close collaboration with the Secretariat of the EAC and benefitted from comments from Charles Omusana, Principal Economist on Investment and Private Sector Promotion. The report has been financially supported by the Government of Finland.

The report was submitted to the OECD Investment Committee for comments on 6 September 2024 and then declassified by the Investment Committee on 11 October 2024.

Table of contents

FIGURES

TABLES

BOXES

Executive summary

The EAC is a very diverse and dynamic regional community offering diverse investment opportunities. FDI inflows to the region have been steadily increasing over the last 20 years, but with strong fluctuations and uneven distribution among Partner States. While the region remains strongly dependent on its natural resources, there is a gradual shift in FDI towards less natural resource-intensive sectors. FDI in the EAC supports job creation and generates spillovers to local economies, but it could further contribute to sustainable development.

The EAC has been at the forefront of regional investment policy making in Africa, with the development of the EAC Model Investment Code in 2006, the EAC Model Investment Treaty in 2016 and the EAC Investment Policy in 2019. The latter was developed to address the challenges needed to improve the investment climate of the region, attract investments and promote the region as a single investment destination. Partner States have also worked to implement these frameworks at the country level and improve their respective investment environments with numerous national initiatives.

The Community is now working on developing the EAC Investment Strategy, which is meant to be the implementation plan for the EAC Investment Policy, and on revising the EAC Model Investment Treaty to adapt it to the recent African Continental Free Trade Agreement (AfCFTA) and its related Investment Protocol. This will necessitate an even greater need to focus on raising the competitiveness of the region for investment and ensuring investment supports sustainable development.

This report introduces newly developed OECD tools and analysis to the EAC region and explores ways to reinvigorate the reform of the EAC investment climate to prepare the region for the AfCFTA, while also providing a greater focus on improving sustainable outcomes from investment. The main messages and considerations are provided below.

Aligning the legal framework for investment to sustainable development objectives

- *Consider revising the EAC Model Investment Treaty to align it with the AfCFTA Investment Protocol*. The EAC Model Investment Treaty extensively incorporates sustainability considerations, though it does not yet fully align with other regional instruments, including with respect to States' commitments and obligations. Reinforcing Partner States' commitment to fostering sustainable investment in the model treaty would contribute to improved clarity and predictability for governments and investors.
- *Increase coherence between national legislation and regional treaties*. The analysis suggests that the EAC Investment Code as well as national investment laws do not yet fully reflect innovations implemented in the EAC Investment Policy. Substantive and procedural elements should be better delineated and additional sustainability-related obligations should be included not only for investors but also for States. This would allow the EAC to create a more enabling yet harmonised business environment, striking the right balance between rights and obligations of investors and EAC Partner States.
- *Entrust EAC bodies with the responsibility of overseeing the implementation of the Investment Code*. Effectively enforcing the EAC Investment Code across all Partner States should be encouraged to the extent possible to realise an enabling, transparent and harmonised regional

investment regime. The non-binding nature of the model code has frequently been cited as a hindrance to FDI inflows in the EAC Investment Policy. An effective approach to accomplishing this goal could involve incentivising the EAC Partner States through offering capacity building and technical assistance in reviewing their laws and entrusting EAC bodies with the responsibility of overseeing the implementation of the Investment Code.

- *Undertake a comprehensive evaluation of the effectiveness and relevance of current regulatory restrictions on FDI in achieving envisioned policy objectives.* By analysing the direct and indirect effects of statutory barriers to FDI on variables such as investment inflows, economic growth, job creation, and sustainable development, policymakers are better enabled to identify any disparities between policy intentions and outcomes. Widespread stakeholder engagement, including with investors, businesses, and civil society, can provide a better understanding of diverse perspectives, informing evidence-based policy adjustments to address challenges posed by existing restrictions.

Promoting and facilitating sustainable investment

- *In line with the EAC Model Investment Code's recommendation, investment promotion agencies (IPAs) should increase their formal interaction with the private sector and other stakeholders, including academia and civil society.* This would strengthen their commitment to investment objectives, gain deeper insight into investor needs and ensure that investment promotion objectives also allow for broader societal benefits. While some EAC IPAs currently include stakeholders in their board of directors, agencies might consider further expanding this representation. Periodic exchanges with other IPAs, including in the context of the upcoming EAC IPA Cooperation Network, would also allow facilitating exchanges and aligning strategies at regional level.
- *As outlined in the EAC Investment Policy, IPAs, could leverage the digital transformation to enhance clarity and policy transparency, reduce the cost of doing business, and facilitate investment information exchange.* Comprehensive information on investment opportunities and procedures should be made easily accessible through their one-stop-shops and online portals. IPAs should also offer sufficient support to facilitate the completion of these procedures in-house. At the regional level, this could be complemented with the establishment of an investors' helpdesk at the EAC Secretariat.
- *While prioritising sustainable FDI represents a commendable initial stride toward achieving the SDGs, IPAs could try to go further by developing and adopting relevant assessment indicators.* These indicators should not be limited to metrics relating to the number and value of investment projects or the number of jobs created. To the extent possible, they must be comprehensive enough to ensure that IPAs attract investments that are aligned with their overarching national development strategy and yield favourable sustainable development outcomes.

Assessing the use and design of investment incentives

- *Consider streamlining and revising the broad offering of corporate income tax incentives to avoid potentially costly redundancies and ensure that incentives are fit-for-purpose and aligned with investment promotion and development objectives.* EAC Partner States offer various tax incentives that benefit almost every sector. Income-based tax incentives are particularly prevalent, despite limited evidence they are effective in mobilising investment for sustainable development. Some countries provide incentives with overlapping sector targeting, allowing investors to benefit from multiple incentives at the same time. Many incentives also target investment projects earning location-based rents (e.g. mining projects), which are less mobile and thus less responsive to incentives. Streamlining and re-designing incentives in a more cost-effective way is in the interest of EAC Partner States, as it can help secure tax revenues for broader investment climate reforms.

But tax competition from peer countries can be a challenge for advancing such reforms. Increasing global and regional co-operation on tax policy matters, such as joining OECD/G20 Inclusive Framework on Base Erosion and Profit Shifting (BEPS) or a transnational forum to create peer-learning opportunities on investment tax incentives, could support countries' transition to smarter and more cost-effective incentives that can better contribute to sustainable development. Collective improvements may also help prevent a race-to-the-bottom in tax incentive competition.

- *Prioritise expenditure-based incentives that are more likely to support investments that would not materialise otherwise.* Expenditure-based incentives (tax allowances and tax credits) are typically more effective in attracting additional investment as they directly reduce the cost of capital of targeted investment expenses and are more cost-transparent as the size of the tax benefit is relative to the amount invested. They are also less likely to erode the 15% global minimum effective tax agreed by the OECD Inclusive Framework. It is encouraging that EAC countries have started using expenditure-based instruments in their incentives mix but most corporate income tax (CIT) incentives in place are still generous exemptions and reduced CIT rates that apply, either for multiple years or permanently, significantly reducing effective tax rates, running against the global minimum tax, and thus subject to potential top-up taxes.
- *Enhance transparency, monitoring and evaluations for a more effective use of incentives.* Increasing transparency of incentive frameworks can benefit investment promotion and foster accountability on the use of public funds. Monitoring and evaluation allows countries to assess whether incentives contribute to policy goals, and at what costs, which can inform decisions on incentive continuity, required amendments and phase outs. The EAC Investment Policy and Partner States already outline information on their tax incentives and engage in tax expenditure reporting. These efforts could be enhanced and complemented by periodical incentive evaluations.

Promoting and enabling responsible business conduct

- *Raise awareness and understanding of responsible business conduct (RBC) and international principles and standards in the field.* The EAC and its Partner States could build on existing initiatives led by some stakeholders to increase knowledge of businesses and other stakeholders about the importance of adopting responsible business practices for sustainable development and build their capacity to conduct risk-based due diligence to identify and address risks of adverse impacts on people, planet, and society. A specific focus could be given to key economic sectors for the region, such as extractive and agriculture, for example, based on the OECD sector-specific Guidance for these two sectors.
- *Encourage responsible business practices at the EAC level across relevant policy areas and promote coherence with international RBC principles and standards.* Taking advantage of the envisaged reform of its investment strategy and Model Investment Code, the EAC could seek to use its investment policies to promote responsible and sustainable investment by integrating considerations and expectations on RBC in these policies. Further, the EAC can leverage its platform to promote the alignment and coordination of policies pertaining to RBC across Partner States, ensuring a common approach aligned with international instruments.
- *Create enabling environments for responsible business practices at the national level.* EAC governments could reinforce their legal and policy frameworks in areas covered by the OECD Guidelines for Multinational Enterprises and take further sector-specific action, in particular to enhance transparency and good governance in the extractive sector. EAC governments could also consider developing and implementing overarching policy frameworks to promote responsible business practices through a whole-of-government approach, such as National Action Plans on RBC or Business and Human Rights.

1 Overview of investment trends and impacts

This chapter provides an overview of recent foreign direct investment (FDI) trends in the EAC, including an assessment of its contribution to sustainable development.

1.1. Introduction: Towards the development of an EAC Investment Strategy

The EAC is a very diverse and dynamic regional economic community (REC) composed of eight Partner States.[1] While the region offers diverse investment opportunities, in part due to its large potential market, vast natural resources and rapid economic expansion, it still lags world averages regarding the attraction of FDI. In most Partner States, the investment rate is below 25% of total GDP, with most of it being driven by domestic investors (UNECA, 2021[1]). In recent years, however, Partner States have taken steps towards improving their investment ecosystem to become a more attractive location for investors. At the same time, like much of Africa, the EAC faces difficulties in attracting FDI, yet such investment is crucial to meeting sustainable development objectives in the region.

According to the African Regional Integration Index, the EAC has the highest level of regional integration among all eight African RECs.[2] The EAC has also been at the forefront of regional investment policy making in Africa, with the EAC Model Investment Code developed in 2006, the EAC Model Investment Treaty in 2016 and, more recently, the EAC Investment Policy (2019-2024) in 2019. The latter has been developed to address the challenges needed to improve the investment climate of the region, attract investments and promote the region as a single investment destination. Partner States have also worked to implement these frameworks at the country level and improve their respective investment environments with numerous national initiatives.

The Community is now working on developing the EAC Investment Strategy, to support the implementation of the EAC Investment Policy, and revising the EAC Model Investment Treaty to adapt it to the AfCFTA and its related Investment Protocol. The latter will offer both greater investment opportunities for the EAC Partner States within an integrated continental market as well as increased competition for footloose investment. This will require a greater need to focus on raising the competitiveness of the region for investment and on improving the sustainable outcomes from investment.

This report introduces newly developed OECD tools and analysis to the EAC region. It is designed as a baseline diagnostic to explore ways to reinvigorate the reform of the EAC investment climate to prepare the region for the AfCFTA, while also providing a greater focus on improving sustainable outcomes from investment.

1.2. FDI trends and contribution to sustainable development in the EAC

1.2.1. FDI in the EAC is growing, albeit modestly, and diversifying beyond natural resources

FDI inflows to the EAC have been steadily increasing over the last 20 years but with strong fluctuations driven by global and regional shocks (Figure 1.2). Following a peak in 2008, FDI plunged in 2009 due to the global financial crisis, as in the rest of the developing economies. Recovery was rapid, however, and FDI reached a new peak in 2012 following the discovery of gas reserves in Tanzania and oil fields in Uganda and the expansion of a large copper and cobalt mine in the Democratic Republic of the Congo (DRC) (UNCTAD, 2013[2]). FDI has been on an upward trend since 2016 which was interrupted only in 2020 by the COVID-19 pandemic from which it rapidly recovered.

FDI inflows to the EAC are unevenly distributed among its members, with three distinct groups. Since 2017 the most resource-rich countries – the DRC, Uganda and Tanzania – have collectively received 79% of total FDI inflows, while Kenya and Rwanda 20%, and Burundi and South Sudan only 1%. Differences also exist in FDI trends over time. While there was an overall upward trend over the last five years, FDI in Kenya declined.

Figure 1.1. FDI flows in the EAC are growing but unevenly distributed across Partner States

FDI net inflows (BoP, current USD billions, % of GDP)

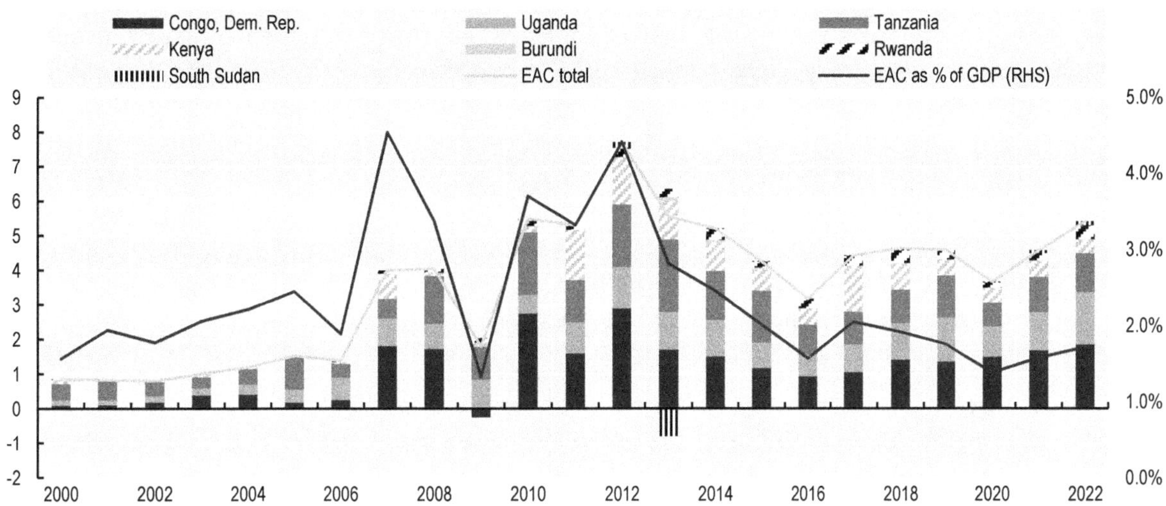

Source: OECD elaboration based on Based on International Monetary Fund (2023[3]), Balance of Payments Statistics.

FDI in the EAC relative to the size of the economy is comparatively similar to that of other regional economic communities (RECs) in Africa (Figure 1.2). During 2017-2022, on average, it represented 1.7% of the bloc's gross domestic product (GDP), higher than in the Economic Community of Western African States (ECOWAS) (1.4%) but just below the Southern African Development Community (SADC) (1.8%) (IMF, 2023[3]). Opportunities for FDI growth in the EAC are significant. Despite representing one-fifth of Africa's population, the seven Partner States have only contributed an average of 10% of the continent's GDP and attracted a mere 11% of FDI inflows to the continent over the past five years (IMF, 2023[3]; IMF, 2023[4]; World Bank, 2023[5]; United Nations, 2022[6]).

Figure 1.2. The performance of FDI inflows in the EAC's economy is comparable to other RECs in Africa

FDI net inflows (BoP, % of GDP)

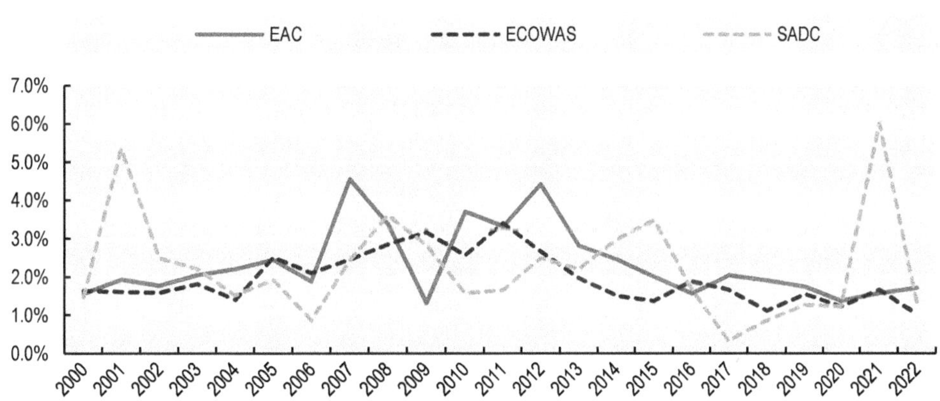

Note: The surge in inflows in 2021 is driven by one large inter-firm transaction in South Africa.
Source: OECD elaboration based on Based on International Monetary Fund (2023[3]), Balance of Payments Statistics.

FDI stock in the EAC generally correlates with the economic size of its Partner States, except for Kenya, the largest economy (Figure 1.3). Yet, when adjusting for the size of the economy, Rwanda is the third most attractive country, with its FDI stock representing 18% of its GDP, after the DRC (31%) and Uganda (25%). The economic importance of FDI stock relative to GDP in the whole region is low, however, averaging 26%. This contrasts sharply with the 70% in SADC – a region with greater natural resources – and the 38% in Africa, yet closely aligns with ECOWAS, which stands at 27% (OECD, 2024[7]; UNCTAD, 2023[8]).

Figure 1.3. A few EAC Partner States have attracted the bulk of FDI stock

Inward FDI Stock, 2022

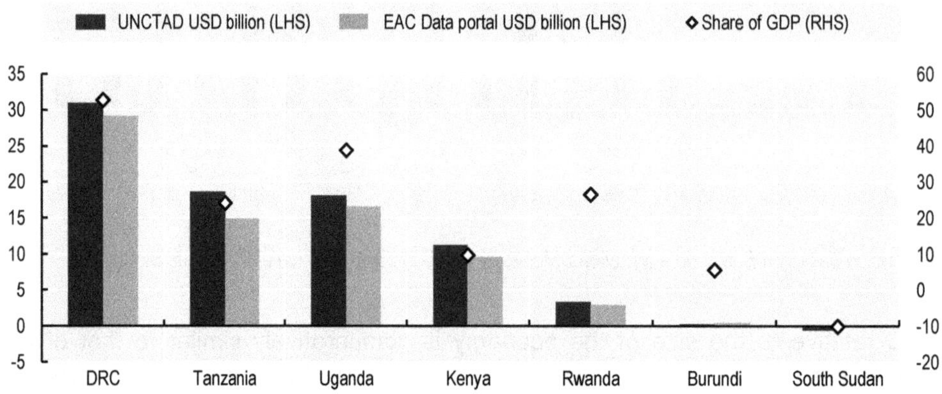

Note: The latest EAC value for the DRC, Rwanda and Tanzania is from 2021. EAC data for South Sudan is unavailable.
Source: OECD elaboration based on UNCTAD (2023[8]) and EAC Data Portal (2023[9]).

Mauritius and South Africa are the leading investors, jointly contributing to 35% of the region's FDI stock in 2022 (Figure 1.4). They are followed by the European Union, which accounts for 25%, followed by China and India (23% combined). The United States, Canada, and the United Kingdom account for 10% collectively and the rest of the world – including notable contributions from Switzerland, Togo, and Nigeria – 9% (IMF, 2023[10]). These results are skewed towards Mauritius because of their high-level of Special Purpose Entities (SPEs) (see note in Figure 1.4). Official EAC data on FDI stock shows Europe as the leading investor, but it only covers Kenya, Tanzania, Rwanda, and Uganda (EAC Data Portal, 2023[9]). For FDI inflows, China and India were the primary investors in the EAC in 2022 (EAC Secretariat, 2023[11]).

The distribution of investments from these principal source economies presents significant variations across the region. Notably, China and India, along with the European Union, allocate approximately 70% of their EAC FDI stocks to the DRC and Kenya. In contrast, the United States, Canada, and the United Kingdom hold a smaller share of 33% in those two countries and allocate 52% of their EAC FDI stock to Tanzania.

Figure 1.4. Most of the FDI in the EAC originates from a small group of countries

FDI Stock by source and host economy in 2022

Note: The Figure is built from outward FDI stocks reported by selected source economies. Direct data was used for Rwanda and Uganda. IMF CDIS data includes Special Purpose Entities (SPEs), which have high levels of pass-through capital—funds that flow through them but originate elsewhere. Excluding FDI associated with these entities would provide a clearer picture of the outward FDI (Angulo and Hierro, 2017[12]).
Source: OECD based on IMF CDIS (2023[10]).

Over the last two decades, greenfield FDI – comprising new FDI projects or expansions of existing FDI – has oscillated between USD 0.5 and 9 billion (Figure 1.5, Panel A). These investment projects have created between 1 000 and 3 000 jobs per year in the region, except in 2019. The recent surge in greenfield FDI flows in 2022 did not result in a proportional increase in job creation, indicating that the new projects are relatively more capital-intensive. The vast majority of the stock of greenfield FDI projects between 2003 and 2022 were in capital-intensive sectors such as electricity and gas (34%), metals (17%), and construction (8%), and related to the region's rich mineral resources and oil and gas reserves (Ministry of Planning DRC, 2020[13]; World Bank, 2023[14]).

Figure 1.5. Greenfield FDI increased and diversified over the last two decades

Greenfield FDI inflows 2003-2022

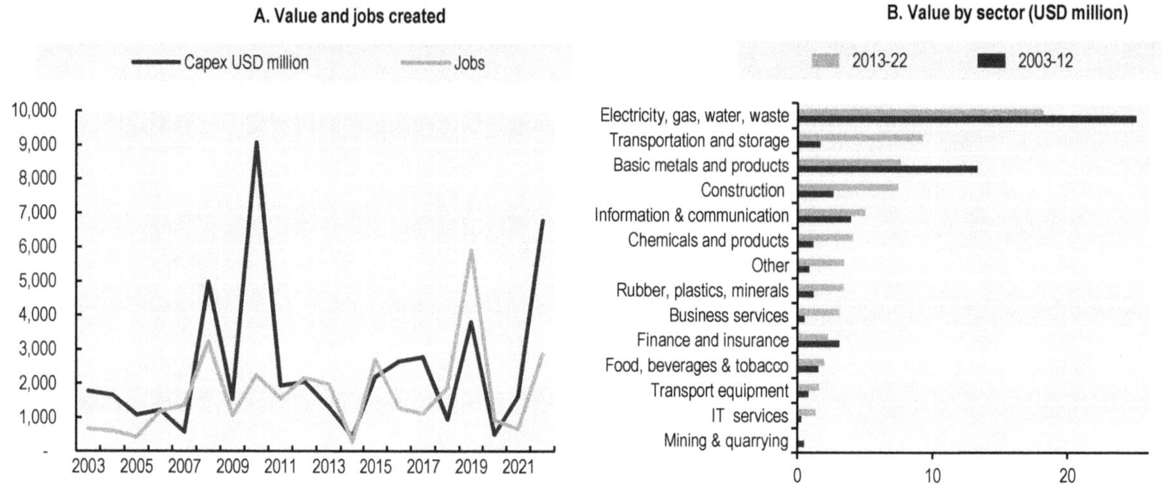

Source: OECD elaboration based on Financial Times fDi Markets (2023[15]).

While the region remains strongly dependent on its natural resources, there is a gradual shift in FDI towards less natural resource intensive sectors, suggesting a move towards more diversification (Figure 1.5, Panel B). Investments in transport, information technology, chemicals, and business services have surged over the past decade (2013-22), while those in electricity, gas, and metals have declined compared to the ten years prior. The extent and direction of this diversification process differs across EAC countries (Figure 1.6). Partner States such as Kenya, Rwanda and Tanzania aligned with the overall trend of diversification. Uganda shifted its greenfield investment focus from energy to services, and South Sudan transitioned towards manufacturing, highlighting a more specialised approach in certain countries.

Figure 1.6. Greenfield FDI inflows sectoral changes differ across countries

Greenfield FDI by broad sector, %

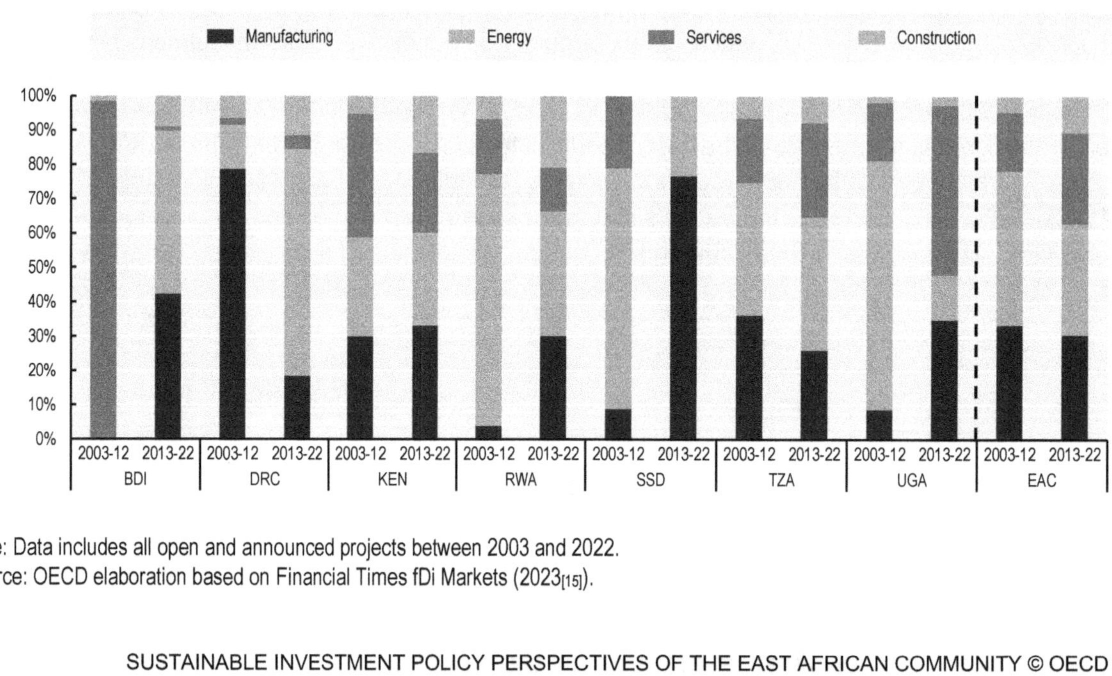

Note: Data includes all open and announced projects between 2003 and 2022.
Source: OECD elaboration based on Financial Times fDi Markets (2023[15]).

1.2.2. FDI in the EAC could further support job creation and sustainable development

FDI has the potential to advance sustainable development, but its impact is not automatic and can vary across countries (OECD, 2022[16]). Greenfield investments created 2.2 jobs per USD million invested in the EAC region, below the world's average of 3 (OECD, 2022[16]). Furthermore, disparities among Partner States persist in this domain. Kenya leads with an average of 3.1 jobs created, followed by Rwanda with 2.8, which is more than double the number in South Sudan, suggesting their higher diversification influences their performance (Figure 1.7).

Manufacturing exhibits the highest job intensity at 1.1 jobs per million, while energy has the lowest at 0.1, reflecting their respective labour and capital-intensive natures. Greenfield FDI in construction and services yield only half as many jobs per million USD as in manufacturing. In Rwanda and Kenya, manufacturing FDI is notably significantly more labour-intensive than elsewhere in EAC. Despite DRC receiving 70% of greenfield investments in manufacturing, job intensity remains low due to 90% of these investments being concentrated in metals. In Uganda and South Sudan, where greenfield FDI in the energy sector is significant, primarily in coal, oil and gas (over 80%), job intensity is the lowest.[3] Typically, FDI in natural resource extraction results in fewer direct jobs (OECD, 2022[16]).

Figure 1.7. The impact of greenfield FDI on job creation strongly varies across EAC countries

Greenfield FDI-induced job creation and sectoral distribution

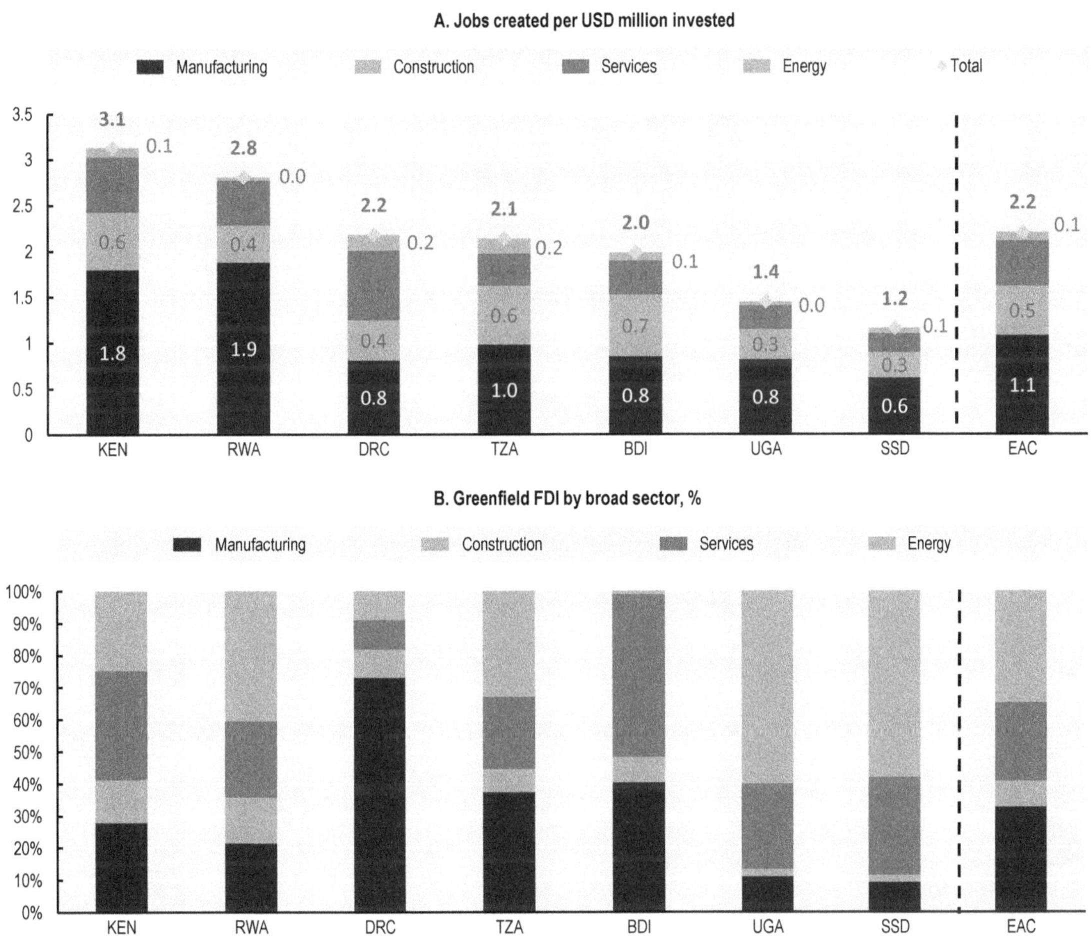

Note: Data includes all open and announced projects between 2003 and 2022.
Source: OECD elaboration based on Financial Times fDi Markets (2023[15]).

Beyond job creation, FDI has the potential to enhance living standards, foster innovation, promote gender equality, and support environmental objectives (OECD, 2022[16]). In the EAC, the levels of wages and training provision underscore the significant role that FDI plays in improving living standards.

Foreign firms are generally more productive than domestic ones (OECD, 2019), a trend observed across the EAC apart from Burundi. On average, foreign firms are three times as productive as domestic ones, with the DRC and Kenya leading in this regard (Figure 1.8, Panel A). Despite this productivity advantage, foreign firms typically pay only 40% higher wages on average. This suggests that the performance premium of foreign firms does not fully translate into wage benefits for workers. Furthermore, foreign firms are offering more training opportunities for their employees, contributing to on-the-job skill development within the region (Figure 1.8, Panel B).

Figure 1.8. FDI plays a significant role in improving living standards and skills

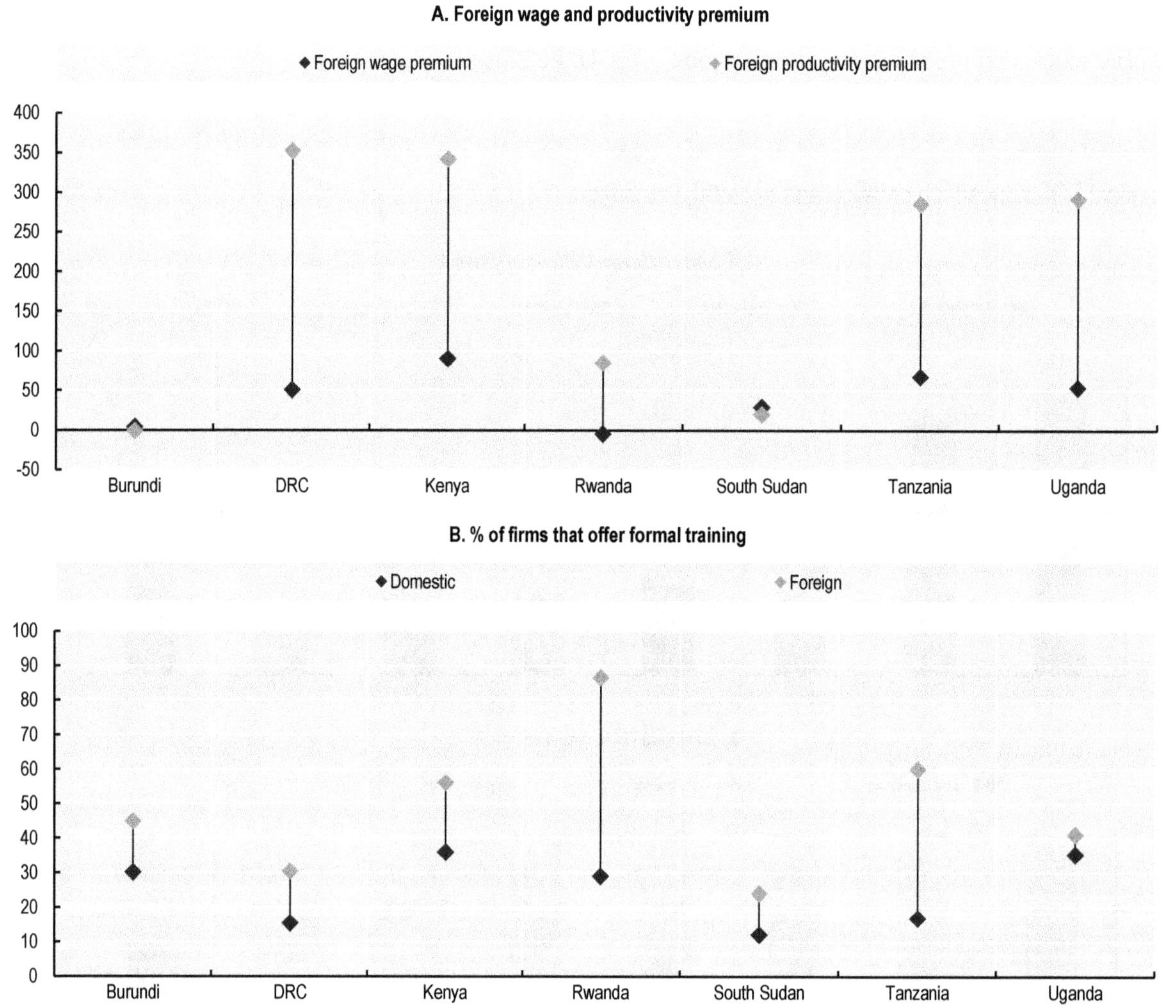

Note: Panel A shows wage and productivity premia of foreign firms in EAC economies. Wage and productivity premia of foreign firms are computed by dividing average wages (productivity) of foreign firms by average wages of domestic firms. Premia above zero imply that foreign firms pay higher wages (are more productive) than domestic firms.
Source: OECD elaboration based on World Bank Enterprise Surveys (2023[17]).

A larger proportion of foreign firms in the EAC introduce new products or services than their domestic counterparts (Figure 1.9, Panel A). Additionally, a higher percentage of foreign firms invest in research and development (R&D) (Figure 1.9, Panel B). These trends suggest a greater innovation capacity among foreign firms, thus offering the potential for knowledge and technology transfer to local businesses.

Figure 1.9. FDI brings innovation and potential spill-overs effects to the local economy

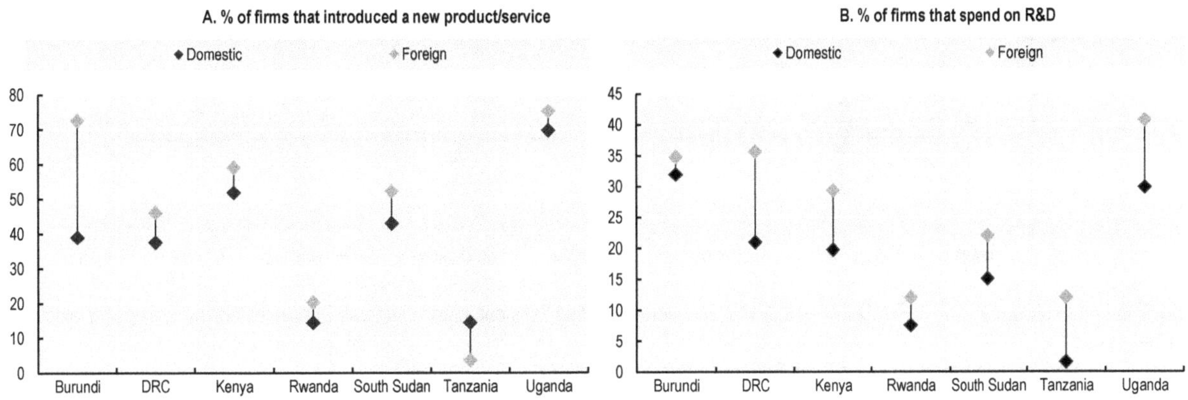

Source: OECD elaboration based on World Bank Enterprise Surveys (2023[17]).

Conversely, the impact of FDI on improving gender equality appears less predominant. Foreign firms in Rwanda and Uganda present a higher proportion of female workers than domestic ones, whereas the gap is negligible in other countries (Figure 1.10, Panel A). Only in Burundi, and minimally in South Sudan, do foreign firms have a higher percentage of female top managers than domestic firms (Figure 1.10, Panel B), yet the gap is not significant, except in Tanzania and Uganda. It is thus not clearcut whether foreign firms are providing more career advancement opportunities for women in the EAC. Similarly, fewer foreign firms have female ownership in the majority of EAC Partner States (Figure 1.10, Panel C).

Figure 1.10. FDI could further advance gender equality

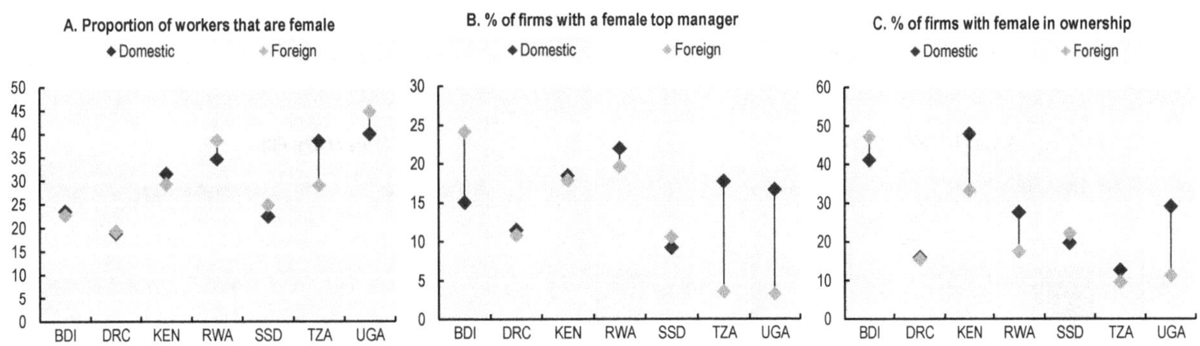

Source: OECD elaboration based on World Bank Enterprise Surveys (2023[17]).

Foreign investors can support a transition to a greener economy through various means. For example, they can bring improvements to the host country in energy efficiency as a result of cleaner or energy-saving technologies (OECD, 2019[18]). In the EAC, manufacturing foreign firms appear to be more energy efficient than domestic firms only in Rwanda and to a lesser extent in Tanzania and Uganda (Figure 1.11).

Figure 1.11. Foreign firms are more energy efficient in only few countries

Are foreign firms more energy efficient than their domestic peers? (yes if value > 0; no if value < 0)

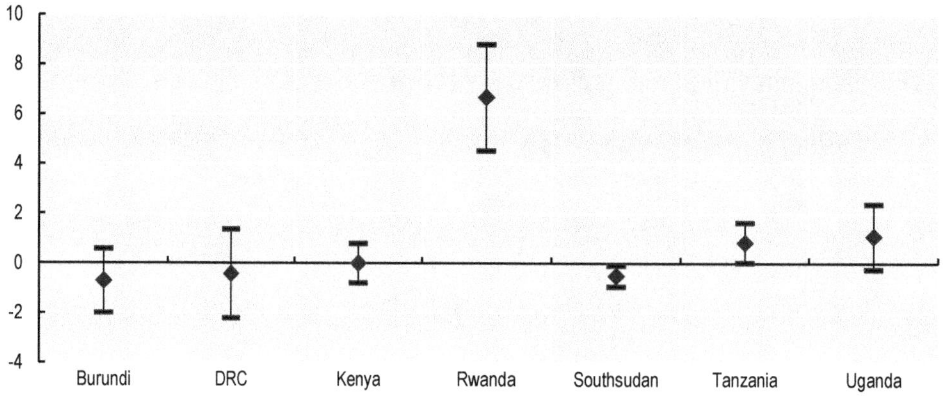

Note: The Figure shows a Type 1 FDI Qualities indicator and corresponding 95% confidence interval. Energy efficiency: sales over electricity and fuel cost.
Source: OECD elaboration based on World Bank Enterprise Surveys (2023[17]).

FDI can also make a significant contribution to the energy transition by increasing renewable energy capacity (OECD, 2022[16]). FDI in renewable energy has gained importance in the EAC, while investment in fossil fuels has declined overall, a trend found in other RECs such as SADC and (OECD, 2023[19]; OECD, 2024[7]). Nevertheless, in East Africa renewable energy accounted for only 4% of greenfield FDI, compared to 17% for Africa as a whole (AUC/OECD, 2023[20]). Despite the higher absolute investment observed in coal, oil, and gas compared to renewable energy, FDI in renewable energy within the region increased substantially by 48% from the period 2003-2012 to 2013-2022, while investment in coal, oil, and gas decreased by 37% over the same period (Figure 1.12, Panel A).

For several EAC nations, FDI in fossil fuels dominates the energy sector, while investments in renewable energies constitute only a small fraction (Figure 1.12, Panel B). Although economies such as Uganda and Tanzania primarily attract FDI in fossil fuels, they have also garnered the majority of FDI in renewables within the region, alongside Kenya, collectively representing 92% of total investment in this sector. This illustrates the current concentration of the sector in a handful of economies.

Figure 1.12. Greenfield FDI in the energy sector is gradually increasing in renewables

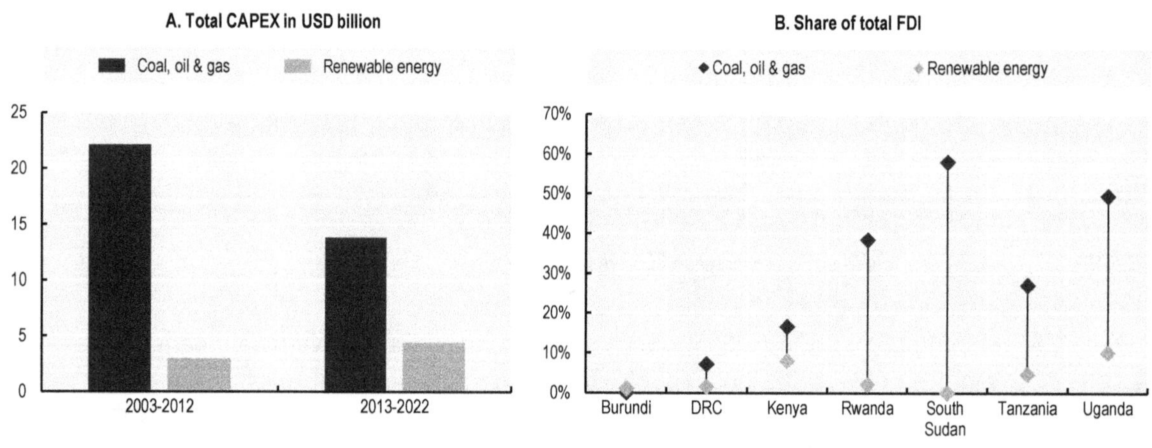

Note: Data includes all open and announced projects between 2003 and 2022.
Source: OECD elaboration based on Financial Times fDi Markets (2023[15]).

References

Angulo, E. and A. Hierro (2017), "Asymmetries in the Coordinated Direct Investment Survey: What Lies Behind?", International Monetary Fund. [12]

AUC/OECD (2023), *Africa's Development Dynamics 2023: Investing in Sustainable Development*, African Union Commission, Addis Ababa/OECD Publishing, Paris, https://doi.org/10.1787/3269532b-en. [20]

EAC Data Portal (2023), *Stock of FDI by Source Region, Million USD, 2022*, https://eac.opendataforafrica.org/fqegwfb/stock-of-fdi-by-source-region-million-usd-2022. [9]

EAC Secretariat (2023), *EAC Trade and Investment Report 2022*, https://www.eac.int/documents/category/trade-investment-reports. [11]

FT fDi Markets (2023), *Database of crossborder greenfield investments*, https://www.fdimarkets.com/ (accessed on 31 January 2024). [15]

IMF (2023), *Balance of Payments and International Investment Position - BOP/IIP Home - IMF Data*, https://data.imf.org/?sk=7a51304b-6426-40c0-83dd-ca473ca1fd52 (accessed on 5 March 2024). [3]

IMF (2023), *Coordinated Direct Investment Survey*, https://data.imf.org/?sk=40313609-f037-48c1-84b1-e1f1ce54d6d5 (accessed on 31 January 2024). [10]

IMF (2023), *World Economic Outlook (October 2023)*, https://www.imf.org/external/datamapper/datasets/WEO (accessed on 31 January 2024). [4]

Ministry of Planning DRC (2020), *Natural Resources and Geographic Profile*, https://www.investindrc.cd/en/Natural-Resources-and-Geographic-Profile#:~:text=Geology,of%20diamonds%2C%20gold%20and%20copper. (accessed on 20 February 2024). [13]

OECD (2024), *Sustainable Investment Policy Perspectives in the Economic Community of West African States (ECOWAS)*, OECD Publishing, Paris, https://doi.org/10.1787/654e2de5-en. [7]

OECD (2023), *Sustainable Investment Policy Perspectives in the Southern African Development Community*, OECD Publishing, Paris, https://doi.org/10.1787/02c9ef1d-en. [19]

OECD (2022), *FDI Quality Indicators 2022*, https://read.oecd-ilibrary.org/view/?ref=1144_1144750-u5ks4jvtnl&title=FDI-Qualities-Indicators-2022 (accessed on 31 January 2024). [16]

OECD (2019), *FDI Qualities Indicators: Measuring the sustainable development impacts of investment*, OECD Publishing, Paris, https://doi.org/10.1787/0894dfba-en. [18]

UNCTAD (2023), *Foreign direct investment: Inward and outward flows and stock, annual (Balance of Payments)*, https://unctadstat.unctad.org/datacentre/dataviewer/US.FdiFlowsStock (accessed on 31 January 2024). [8]

UNCTAD (2013), *World Investment Report 2013: Global Value Chains: Investment and Trade for Development*, https://unctad.org/system/files/official-document/wir2013_en.pdf. [2]

UNECA (2021), *Investing in Eastern Africa: Opportunities and Challenges*, https://www.uneca.org/sites/default/files/SROs/Presentation%20Study%20on%20UNECA%20ICSOE%202021%20Investing%20in%20Eastern%20Africa.pdf. [1]

United Nations (2022), *World Population Prospects 2022*, https://population.un.org/dataportal/home?df=2ea9d0d7-ba7c-497d-a2bc-2847820fe391 (accessed on 31 January 2024). [6]

World Bank (2023), *Democratic Republic of Congo Overview: Development news, research, data | World Bank*, https://www.worldbank.org/en/country/drc/overview#1 (accessed on 21 February 2024). [14]

World Bank (2023), *World Bank Enterprise Survey*, https://www.enterprisesurveys.org/en/enterprisesurveys (accessed on 31 January 2024). [17]

World Bank (2023), *World Development Indicators*, https://databank.worldbank.org/source/world-development-indicators (accessed on 31 January 2024). [5]

Notes

[1] The EAC Partner States are the Democratic Republic of the Congo, the Federal Republic of Somalia, the Republic of Burundi, the Republic of Kenya, the Republic of Rwanda, the Republic of South Sudan, the Republic of Uganda, and the United Republic of Tanzania. Somalia is not included in the analysis in this report as it had not yet formally joined the EAC when the report was being prepared.

[2] The African Regional Integration Index was jointly developed by the African Union, the African Development Bank and the United Nations Economic Commission for Africa. See: https://www.integrate-africa.org/.

[3] These results use FDI Markets data from 2003-2022. According to the EAC Trade and Investment Report 2022, FDI in energy, including mining, quarrying, and utilities, accounted for only 14% of the total in Uganda from 2017 to 2022, reflecting a shift towards services (EAC Secretariat, 2023[11]). Data on South Sudan was not available.

2 Aligning the legal framework for investment to sustainable development objectives

This chapter provides an overview of recent foreign direct investment (FDI) trends in the EAC, including an assessment of its contribution to sustainable development

Sustainability outcomes have become a primary consideration in investment policy making, and legal regimes for investment are increasingly focused on fostering sustainable development. As such, sustainability language is more frequently incorporated into investment legal frameworks – which consist of the domestic legal framework (investment and related laws), and international treaties that offer additional provisions and protections to foreign investors.

In line with this trend, EAC Partner States are progressively addressing sustainability considerations in their international and regional instruments as well as in their domestic laws. The EAC Investment Policy elaborated in November 2019 confirms EAC's willingness to further embed sustainability commitments into its legal instruments. As it stands, EAC's Model Investment Treaty seeks "*to promote, facilitate, encourage, protect and increase investment opportunities that enhance sustainable development within the territories of the State Parties*" (EAC, 2016[1]). The African Union, including the EAC Partner States, also adopted in 2023 the Investment Protocol to the Agreement establishing the African Continental Free Trade Area on Investment (AfCFTA Investment Protocol) – likely marking a pivotal moment in investment policymaking. Advancements brought by the AfCFTA Investment Protocol have prompted discussions on the alignment between regional and national initiatives, including domestic investment laws.

This section provides an analysis to compare innovations at the regional and continental levels with domestic laws and regulations and assesses coherence between action at the national and regional levels. The analysis below suggests that the EAC Model Investment Treaty extensively incorporates sustainability considerations, albeit not as much as the AfCFTA and the Draft Pan African Investment Code (PAIC). This analysis also shows the level of regulatory restrictions to FDI adopted by the EAC Partner States. It then demonstrates that the EAC Investment Code and national investment laws do not yet fully reflect innovations at a regional level, although recent legislations are seemingly more aligned with regional practices.

2.1. International regime for investment protection has become a cause for concern

Historically, international investment agreements (IIAs), including regional agreements and bilateral investment treaties (BITs), were seen as tools to safeguard investors and investments and to stimulate FDI, by enhancing the predictability of the applicable legal framework and mitigating undue risks for investors. These agreements form a significant component of a state's investment climate.

IIAs offer both substantive and procedural protections to foreign investors. Common substantive protections include safeguards against unlawful expropriation and discrimination – including through provisions such as national treatment (NT) and most favoured nation (MFN) – and guarantees of fair and equitable treatment (FET) and full protection and security (FPS). Enforcement of these obligations often includes investor-state dispute settlement (ISDS) mechanisms, allowing investors to bring claims against the host state in which they have invested before international arbitral tribunals in the event of breach of the IIAs.

Many IIAs were designed decades ago with a different global economy and concerns in mind – as such, some doubts have emerged about the design of some of these treaties, their interpretation, and the use of certain clauses (OECD, 2024[2]). One of these concerns pertains to the growing number of ISDS cases over the past decade, often regarding public policy or regulatory measures, resulting in concerns about a potential freezing effect on regulations to avoid future disputes. Governments are increasingly intent on reshaping investment treaties to revisit their role, purpose and content. While some countries, such as India, Indonesia and South Africa have terminated their investment treaties, others are working to improve their treaty system. The Future of Investment Treaties work programme hosted by the OECD examines new trends and developments in treaty design, focusing on the one hand on to what extent alignment may exist between IIAs and the 2015 Paris Agreement and on the other hand on whether and how to bring change to substantive provisions in earlier generation IIAs to better align them with current designs.[1] The United Nations Commission on International Trade Law (UNCITRAL) is also working on a comprehensive reform of the ISDS system.

2.2. Towards an innovative and transparent regional investment regime in Africa

African States have been very active in reshaping their treaty system and have devised innovative approaches to address growing concerns with respect to IIAs (OECD, 2024[3]). These innovations can be found in the EAC Model Investment Treaty as well as in the non-binding PAIC, the AfCFTA Investment Protocol and in regional instruments such as the SADC Model BIT (OECD, 2023[4]). These instruments incorporate sustainable development considerations and contain innovative provisions on various policy issues. They demonstrate States' readiness to enhance their investment framework in an attempt to further attract investments that foster sustainable development, to redefine the scope of substantive protections in line with recent practices (OECD, 2024[2]), to preserve the State's right to regulate, to commit on sustainable development-related issues and to redesign the ISDS mechanisms in place.

This section reviews developments in the following regional and continental approaches, with a focus on the alignment of the EAC Model Investment Treaty with other regional and continental instruments:

- The EAC Model Investment Treaty adopted by EAC Partner States adopted in February 2016;
- The AfCFTA Investment Protocol, adopted by member states of the African Union (including EAC Partner States) in February 2023;[2] and
- The draft PAIC, discussed by member states of the African Union (including EAC Partner States) in December 2016.

2.2.1. Extensive considerations of sustainability in the preamble and general provisions of all three instruments

The EAC Model Investment Treaty, the AfCFTA Investment Protocol and the PAIC all extensively incorporate considerations of sustainability, including in their respective preambles. The EAC Model Investment Treaty generally aligns with other continental instruments in that respect, though some definitions contained therein, such as that of the term investment, could be further refined to fully mirror the practices of the African Union.

The EAC Model Investment Treaty recognises the role of investment in fostering sustainable development – including through the reduction of poverty, the increase of productive capacity and economic growth. Sustainable development is moreover enshrined in the objective provision of the EAC Model Investment Treaty. The PAIC and the AfCFTA Investment Protocol contain similar language both in their respective preamble and other general provisions including in the objective provision, but the AfCFTA Investment Protocol goes further than other instruments by exhorting investors to "*endeavour to achieve the highest possible level of contribution to sustainable development*" (AfCFTA, 2023[5]) of the host State. All three instruments reaffirm States' right to regulate and seek to achieve a better balance between investors and states' rights and obligations.

All three instruments define protected investments, though definitions provided in the AfCFTA Investment Protocol and the PAIC are more comprehensive than those of the EAC Model Investment Treaty. For instance, under Article 1 of the AfCFTA Investment Protocol, an investment "*must have the following characteristics: commitment of capital or other resources, the expectation of gain or profit, a certain duration, assumption of risk, and a significant contribution to the Host State's sustainable development*" (AfCFTA, 2023[5]). By contrast, the EAC Model Investment Treaty does not outline the characteristics of a protected investment in the article dedicated to definitions. It nevertheless provides, in a separate article, that an enterprise with "*no substantial business activities*" (EAC, 2016[1]) in the territory of the host state may be denied the benefit of protection provided therein (art. 19 EAC Model Investment Treaty). In practice, this means that efforts to establish an investment are not protected under the agreement until a substantial business activity exists in the territory of the host state; only then would the investment qualify as a protected investment. For the sake of clarity, the EAC Model Investment Treaty could incorporate clear characteristics in the definition of (protected) investments and consider defining its components. The instruments identify exclusions to protected investments, such as portfolio investment, presumably affirming the states' desire to attract more substantial investments that may have a more positive contribution to sustainable development.

2.2.2. The instruments all contain more concise and transparent substantive provisions to advance sustainable development

Insights gained from investment arbitration and evolving societal expectations have prompted States to adjust their treaty policy, including by better delineating standards of protection provided therein. The three instruments examined, including the EAC Model Investment Treaty, are all aligned in that respect, as they all contain precisely defined substantive standards of protection, in line with more recent treaty practices (OECD, 2024[2]).

The three instruments analysed all contain detailed provisions on non-discrimination (including NT and MFN provisions) and exceptions thereto. They unanimously define the component of "*like circumstances*", necessary when assessing the application of NT and MFN, and list examples of elements that should be examined for their application in line with recent treaty practices (*see e.g.* art. 12 AfCFTA Investment Protocol). These provisions do not extend to the pre-establishment phase of investments – as evidenced by the use of terms such as "*management*", "*conduct*" and "*disposition*" in relevant provisions (*see e.g.* art. 4 EAC Model Investment Treaty). Exceptions to NT in the AfCFTA Investment Protocol and the PAIC include measures taken by a state to protect or enhance legitimate public policy objectives and preferential treatment to achieve national development activities. The EAC Model Investment Treaty also provides for exclusions to NT, though by reference to schedules to be included in due course; it nonetheless recognises the possibility of preferential treatment to achieve national or regional goals in a separate article dedicated to the State's right to pursue development goals. All three instruments exclude from their respective MFN provision treatment promised under other investment treaties (*see e.g.* art. 5 EAC Model Investment Treaty).

In line with recent treaty practices (OECD, 2021[6]), guarantees against unlawful expropriation (including indirect expropriation) are provided in all three instruments, as well as methods to determine the value of the compensation (*see e.g.* art. 7 EAC Model Investment Treaty). Exclusions to this guarantee consistently include measures taken to protect or enhance legitimate public welfare objectives, usually pertaining to sustainable development goals (*see e.g.* art. 20 and subsequent AfCFTA Investment Protocol).

None of the three instruments include traditional FET provision. Like the AfCFTA Investment Protocol, the EAC Model Investment Treaty adopts a restrictive approach to the treatment of investors and investments, to the extent that States have the obligation to ensure that their administrative, legislative and judicial processes are not arbitrary and protect against denial of justice and due process. The AfCFTA Investment Protocol provides for a similar obligation under the term of "*Administrative and Judicial treatment*" and protects investors against, *inter alia*, denial of justice, denial of due process and discrimination based on gender (AfCFTA, 2023[5]). Both these instruments define the contours of the '*fair*' and '*equitable*" treatment through a closed list (OECD, 2023[7]).

Similar to the AfCFTA Investment Protocol, the EAC Model Investment Treaty contains a separate provision reaffirming the State's right to regulate, including the right to take measures ensuring that investment is consistent with goals of sustainable development and social and economic policy objectives (*see e.g.* art. 15 EAC Model Investment Treaty); in the case of the AfCFTA Investment Protocol this provision is included under the "*Sustainable development-related issues*" chapter (AfCFTA, 2023[5]). Specific exclusions to various investor protections are also contained in these instruments, including when measures seek to protect the environment (*see e.g.* art. 8 EAC Model Investment Treaty), or to comply with the State's international obligations – *a fortiori* including those related to sustainable development (*see e.g.* art 24 AfCFTA Investment Protocol).

2.2.3. Considerable efforts have been made to rebalance the rights and obligations of investors on a continental scale

All three instruments examined strive to rebalance the rights and obligations provided to investors in IIAs, by including investors' obligations, such as those that relate to sustainable development, even though investors are not parties to the agreements. Nevertheless, while the AfCFTA Investment Protocol and the PAIC dedicate a separate chapter to investors' obligations, those under the EAC Model Investment Treaty are scattered across the text. More generally, the EAC Model Investment Treaty is often more succinct when it comes to investors' obligations than other instruments.

In substance, all instruments require investors to comply with domestic laws and regulations (*see e.g.* art. 10 EAC Model Investment Treaty) and prohibit them from engaging in corruption (as the author or the accomplice) both pre and post establishment (*see e.g.* art. 11 EAC Model Investment Treaty).

Under all three instruments, investors are required to respect and protect the environment when carrying out their activity and to restore the environment (to the extent feasible) in the event of damage. The EAC Model Investment Treaty is relatively succinct on environmental obligations of investors. By contrast, the AfCFTA Investment Protocol is the most comprehensive in addressing investors' obligations with respect to environmental protection and dedicates a stand-alone provision to that effect, listing different types of obligations. Both the AfCFTA Investment Protocol and the PAIC enjoin investors to carry out environmental impact assessments and the EAC Model Investment Treaty encourages the development of adequate new green technologies. The EAC Model Investment Treaty and the PAIC further allow States to impose requirements on investors through the lifecycle of the investment to enhance its benefits (*e.g.* enhance productive capacity, increase employment, new technologies).

All three instruments require investors to comply with labour and human rights regulations (*see e.g.* art. 16 EAC Model Investment Treaty). Contrary to other instruments, the EAC Model Investment Treaty does not include obligations of corporate social responsibility The AfCFTA Investment Protocol further compels investors to respect the rights and dignity of indigenous people and local communities. All instruments establish the obligation for investors to comply with international conventions and policies on labour, including those relating to child labour (*see e.g.* art. 16 EAC Model Investment Treaty).

Instruments studied unanimously encourage investors to adopt practices that allow the transfer and rapid diffusion of technologies and know-how (*see e.g.* art. 30 AfCFTA Investment Protocol).

In light of the above, strengthening investors' obligations where necessary and compiling them in a single chapter would allow the EAC to further align its instruments with the practices of the African Union.

LIke the AfCFTA Investment Protocol and the PAIC, the EAC Model Investment Treaty remains silent as to the consequences of a breach by an investor of their obligations. Various consequences can therefore be drawn based on dispute settlement provisions. Indeed, similarly to the PAIC, the EAC Model Investment Treaty allows States to bring a counterclaim against the investor in dispute settlement proceedings in the event of a breach by the latter of their obligations. The PAIC however expressly allows for the possibility of a set off if the breach is materially relevant to the issue before the competent body. Monetary liability of the investor is also recognised in the EAC Model Investment Treaty (civil action before domestic courts), similarly to the PAIC (any competent body dealing with a dispute under the code). In the specific case of corruption activities, the EAC Model Investment Treaty is also silent as to the consequences of such breach. By contrast, the AfCFTA Investment Protocol explicitly deems that a breach of the anti-corruption provision amounts to a breach of the domestic laws and regulations, therefore amounting to a breach of the protocol itself.

2.2.4. State commitments and obligations concerning key sustainable development matters in the EAC Model Investment Treaty are not fully aligned with continental practices

All instruments contain obligations and commitments for the state parties concerning key sustainable development matters, including on environment, labour, human rights and corruption. The AfCFTA Investment Protocol and the PAIC are particularly detailed and set out a broad range of commitments and obligations for members, while the EAC Model Investment Treaty is relatively succinct on the issue. All instruments explicitly require state parties not to lower certain standards in encouraging investment: the EAC Model Investment Treaty prohibits state parties from relaxing or waiving environmental and labour legislations, whereas the two other instruments go further, one by including a reference to "*environment, labour and consumer protection laws and international minimum standards*" (art. 25, (AfCFTA, 2023[5])) and the other by referring to the "*protection of human, animal or plant life or health*" (art. 14, (PAIC, 2016[8])).

All three instruments compel state parties to ensure the protection of the environment; the AfCFTA Investment Protocol further includes a provision specifically dedicated to climate change, requiring state parties to take action to promote their climate change policies.

State parties are also prompted, to varying degrees, to establish national policies to guide investors in developing human capacity of the labour force (including policies focused on the special needs of the youth, women, and other vulnerable groups). The AfCFTA also requires state parties to promote and enforce laws and policies to protect, *inter alia*, the rights of indigenous peoples and local communities.

The AfCFTA Investment Protocol and the PAIC touch upon health considerations and compel state parties to promote and facilitate investment in the public health sector (art. 27 AfCFTA Investment Protocol) or to take measures to protect the health, safety and economic interests of consumers (art. 40 PAIC). By contrast, while the EAC Model Investment Treaty recognises in its preamble that the objective of the treaty can be achieved without compromising, *inter alia*, health measures and safety measures, it does not include any commitments by the Partner States with respect to this topic.

Tellingly, only the AfCFTA Investment Protocol reaffirms state parties' obligation to promote and enforce anti-corruption, anti-money laundering, anti-terrorism financing and anti-bribery measures.[3]

All three instruments include various other commitments and obligations for member parties which could also affect sustainable development, such as the obligation to facilitate investment that contributes to sustainable development (including through the assistance of existing IPAs, the obligation to support the provision of technical assistance, capacity building and co-operation or the obligation to ensure the transparency of information).

2.2.5. Innovative dispute settlement and alternatives to traditional ISDS mechanisms are incorporated in all instruments

In response to mounting scepticism of the reliability of ISDS mechanisms, all three instruments explore, to varying degrees, novel and innovative reforms to ISDS. These approaches entail either excluding an enforcement mechanism altogether, or, if retained, adding specific conditions such as prior consultations, conciliation or mediation, exhaustion of domestic remedies or cooling-off periods. The EAC Model Investment Treaty expressly discourages the inclusion of ISDS mechanisms in final versions of IIAs.

The EAC Model Investment Treaty prescribes recourse to arbitration in the event of a state-to-state dispute where (i) a state is claiming damages on behalf of an investor for a breach of the treaty (subject, *inter alia*, to the claim not being time-barred as per the treaty), or (ii) a dispute arose between the state parties concerning the interpretation of the application thereof (subject, *inter alia*, to prior recourse to amicable dispute resolution mechanisms). The EAC Model Investment Treaty stands out from other continental instruments by discouraging the inclusion of ISDS mechanisms. If included, recourse to ISDS must be conditioned upon prior amicable dispute resolution mechanisms, exhaustion of local remedies and preceded by a cooling off period of six months. Moreover, the ISDS provision included in the IIA (in its final version) is overridden if the investment contract contains a dispute resolution clause and when the underlying measure in the ISDS would be covered by such a dispute resolution clause. Recourse to arbitration is also confined to a period of three years as of the knowledge of the breach which is the object of the dispute.

The EAC Model Investment Treaty does not contain express provisions requiring state parties to facilitate the prevention of disputes and management of grievances – unlike in the AfCFTA Investment Protocol. Yet, establishing such a mechanism is often considered a key building block of a robust aftercare and retention strategy and is crucial in avoiding costs associated with ISDS.[4] The inclusion of a specific provision of dispute prevention and avoidance in the EAC Model Investment Treaty, in line with the AfCFTA Investment Protocol, is therefore encouraged.

The PAIC's approach to dispute resolution is also noteworthy: recourse to ISDS is left to the discretion of member states, which is arguably "*a middle ground solution to African States that are either pro-ISDS or anti-ISDS*" (Mbengue and Schacherer, 2021[9]). Should they choose to do so, parties to the dispute shall first seek to resolve the dispute, within six months at the latest, though consultation and negotiations. Recourse to ISDS is also conditioned upon the exhaustion of local remedies. The PAIC also contains a fork in the road provision, which implies that the choice of forum is final and irrevocable.

2.3. Balancing sustainable development needs with non-discrimination

2.3.1. EAC Partner States are generally more restrictive than other developing and emerging economies

An open and non-discriminatory international investment environment can offer considerable long-term advantages, serving as a potential catalyst for economic growth and sustainable development. By raising an economy's attractiveness to FDI, it can contribute to enhancing the economy's productive capacity and capital allocation efficiency, and foster job creation and income growth. Despite the widespread recognition of these benefits, governments worldwide often impose legal constraints on foreign investors' entry and operations. These restrictions can sometimes serve legitimate policy objectives: promoting domestic firms and protecting them from foreign competition, particularly SMEs or infant industries; encouraging technology transfers through joint ventures; or safeguarding national sovereignty, particularly regarding essential security interests. But such restrictions may not always be the best means to achieve these objectives, and they come at a potential cost. FDI restrictions should thus be employed judiciously after careful consideration of their potential deterrent effect on FDI inflows, which can ultimately lead to diminished competition and market contestability, forgone government revenues, and reduced opportunities for knowledge spillovers and productivity gains.

Despite substantial liberalisation worldwide over time, most governments continue to discriminate against foreign investors to a more or lesser extent. The *OECD FDI Regulatory Restrictiveness Index* (FDI Index) offers a means for comparing statutory FDI restrictions in over 100 nations, categorised into four main types, but it does not assess to what extent these statutory restrictions are exercised in practice (Box 2.1). Considerable diversity in FDI restrictiveness is evident among countries and regions, where OECD economies typically are less restrictive on average while some larger or resource-rich economies tend to adopt more stringent regulations. Policy stances also differ across regions, with those countries in the Middle East and North Africa and Asia-Pacific regions tending to be relatively more restrictive overall.

Box 2.1. OECD FDI Regulatory Restrictiveness Index

The OECD FDI Regulatory Restrictiveness Index (FDI Index) seeks to gauge the restrictiveness of a country's FDI rules. The FDI Index is currently available for over 100 countries. It is not a standalone measure of a country's investment climate since it does not cover many other aspects of the investment regulatory framework or the actual implementation of formal restrictions. But FDI rules are a critical determinant of FDI attractiveness and help to explain the varied performance across countries in attracting FDI (Mistura and Roulet, 2019[10]).

The FDI Index covers 22 sectors, including agriculture, mining, electricity, manufacturing and main services (transport, construction, distribution, communications, real estate, financial and professional services). Restrictions are evaluated on a 0 (open) to 1 (closed) scale following a standardised policy scoring framework, and common sectors weights, reflecting their average share in total value added over the years 1995, 2000, 2005, 2010 and 2015 for 64 economies included in the OECD Input-Output Tables, are applied across countries to compute sector scores (Mistura, forthcoming[11]). The overall country FDI Index score is the sum of the 22 sector sectors. Where a measure is applicable to only a sub-set of activities in a sector or sub-sector, scores are adjusted to account for its limitation in scope and thus degree of restrictiveness.

For each sector, the scoring is based on the following policy elements:

- the level of foreign equity ownership permitted;
- the screening/approval procedures applied to inward foreign direct investment;
- restrictions on key foreign personnel; and
- other restrictions, e.g. on land ownership, reciprocity requirement, discriminatory minimum capital and local content requirements and public procurement practices.

Measures considered by the FDI Index are limited to statutory restrictions on FDI. Actual enforcement and implementation procedures are not assessed. The discriminatory nature of measures, i.e. when they apply to foreign investors only, is the central criterion for scoring a measure. State ownership and state monopolies, to the extent they do not discriminate against foreigners, are not scored. Preferential treatment for special economic zones and export-oriented investors is also not factored into the score, nor is the more favourable treatment of one group of investors because of preferential treatment under international agreements.

Source: https://www.oecd.org/en/topics/investment.html.

On average, EAC countries are more restrictive than most other countries covered by the Index, with some outliers (Figure 2.1). Uganda's foreign investment restrictions align more closely with the average level observed in OECD countries, whereas Rwanda imposes fewer restrictions than the OECD average. Conversely, Tanzania's restrictions are nearly double the level observed in non-OECD countries, with Kenya, the DRC, and Burundi falling somewhere in between.

The top scores of the most restrictive EAC countries mainly stem from broad-based horizontal restrictions imposed on almost all foreign investors across various sectors. This trend is particularly pronounced in Tanzania, where horizontal restrictions extend to accessing local financing, favouring local firms in public procurement, and imposing barriers on unconditional profit and capital repatriation. Across the region, foreign investors are also typically confronted with horizontal discriminatory rules on access to land for business purposes and public procurement, which are evident in nearly all EAC Partner States.

The prevalence of horizontal measures such as restrictions on access to land, local preference during government procurement, and minimum capital thresholds can significantly affect the attractiveness of the manufacturing sector, a sector often prioritised in the EAC. Restrictions on land access can hinder foreign investors' ability to secure suitable sites for manufacturing facilities, potentially delaying or deterring investment altogether. Moreover, requirements for local preference in government procurement may limit the market opportunities for foreign-owned manufacturers, reducing their competitiveness compared to locally-owned firms while minimum capital thresholds can pose financial barriers to entry for foreign investors, especially smaller or newer enterprises, limiting their ability to establish or expand manufacturing operations.

Foreign equity limits in specific economic activities and/or sectors are also widely used by EAC countries (see Annex A). This type of restriction is also common in many other regions. It has the advantage of being relatively easy to administer and is assumed to be able to fulfil several policy objectives at once, e.g. preserving to some extent local competitors, contributing to technology transfer, and allowing domestic investors to share rents with their foreign partners. Sometimes the option of a local partner is appealing for investors, where there are high fixed start-up costs or where local knowledge is an advantage, such as in the food or retail sectors. However, the empirical evidence suggests that foreign shareholding limitations tend to discourage FDI overall (Mistura and Roulet, 2019[10]). Foreign investors seem to have a clear preference for holding full or majority-ownership of their investments abroad, which allows control over their operations.[5]

Figure 2.1. EAC Partners States in the OECD FDI Regulatory Restrictiveness Index, 2021

(open=0, closed=1)

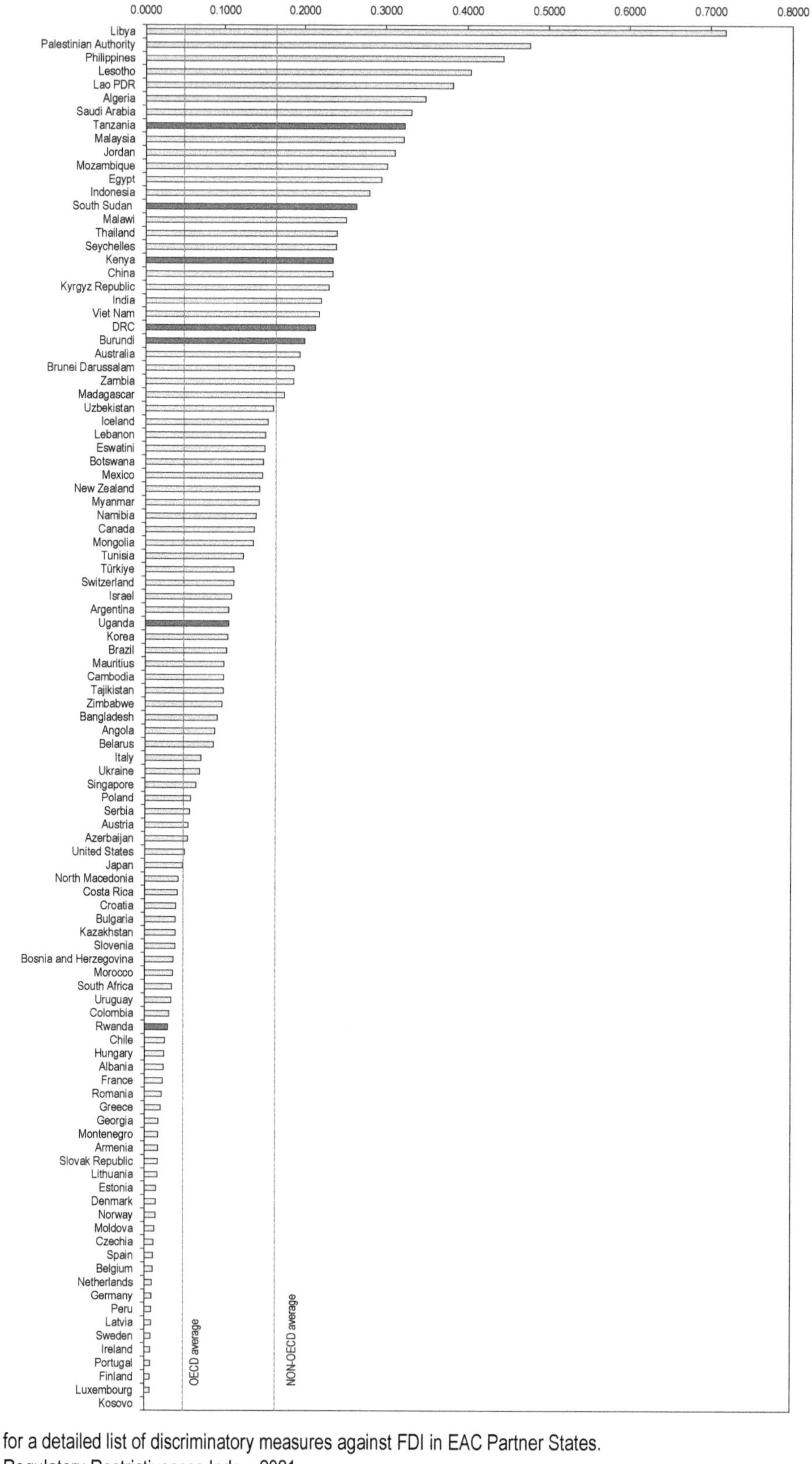

Note: See Annex A for a detailed list of discriminatory measures against FDI in EAC Partner States.
Source: OECD FDI Regulatory Restrictiveness Index, 2021.

The DRC is the only country with substantial discriminatory restrictions on foreign key personnel and with overall investment screening. Investment screening is becoming more prevalent in both OECD and non-OECD countries, driven primarily by considerations of national security rather than for economic reasons.

Where restrictions are not horizontal, the extent of regulation varies across sectors (Figure 2.2). Real estate investment emerges as the most tightly controlled activity in the region, with foreign investors being frequently subject to more stringent rules than domestic investors regarding land and real estate ownership rights (e.g., being sometimes allowed only to invest in land and real estate assets through leasing arrangements while domestic investors are entitled to fully own such as through freehold titles).[6] Similarly, restrictions on foreign ownership of agricultural land are prevalent, as they are in many countries, particularly in Asia. Certain countries also reserve construction services exclusively for nationals, while others may grant foreign nationals temporary licences for specific construction projects, such as in Tanzania. In Kenya, admission of foreign construction firms hinges on the value of the construction projects, and if the threshold is met, the foreign company must either subcontract or form a joint venture with local ownership comprising at least 30%.

Figure 2.2. FDI restrictions by sector, EAC regional average vs OECD and non-OECD averages

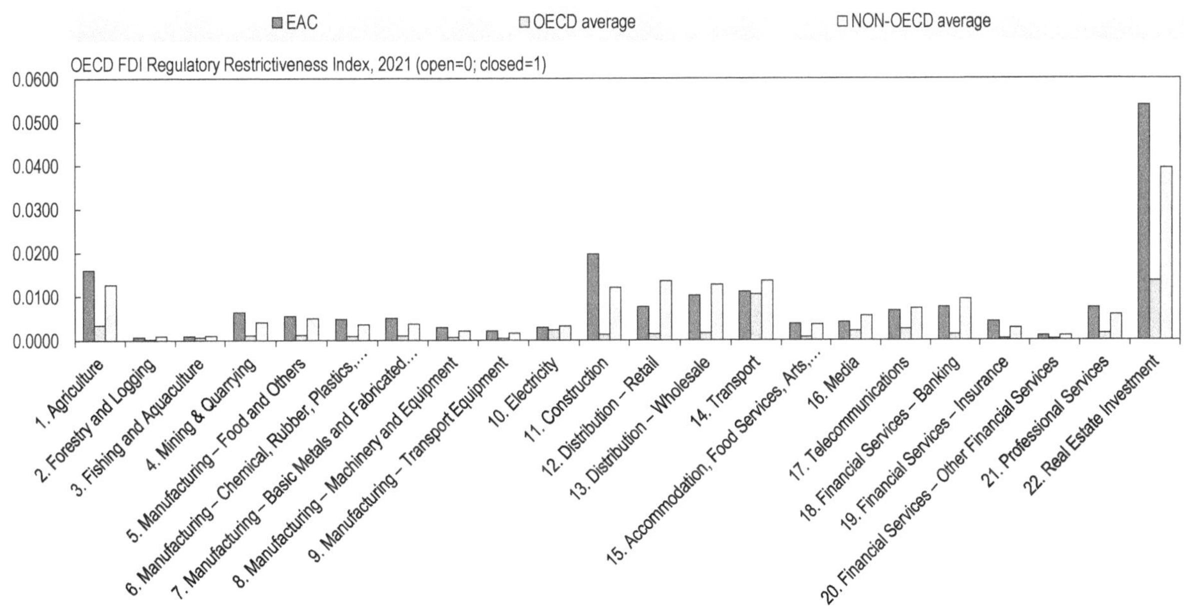

Note: See Annex A for a detailed list of discriminatory measures against FDI in EAC Partner States.
Source: OECD FDI Regulatory Restrictiveness Index, 2021.

Several countries in the region have actively been liberalising their investment regulations, particularly since 2021. For instance, Kenya abolished a 30% local shareholding requirement in the telecommunications sector in 2023, reversing its previous decision to raise the threshold from 20% to 30% in 2020. Kenya had also eliminated a strong barrier in 2015, when it abolished a 75% cap on foreign ownership in listed companies. Additionally, in 2022, Rwanda removed local content requirements for radio broadcasters and free-to-air licensees, facilitating increased foreign investment in the media sector. Similarly, Uganda opened its fishing sector in 2023 by removing nationality requirements for obtaining fishing licences. In contrast, Uganda has tightened restrictions in its mining sector in 2022, limiting licences for artisanal and small-scale mining activities to Ugandan citizens or companies wholly owned by Ugandan nationals. Future updates of the FDI Index would allow EAC Partner States to showcase their reforms to the international community.

2.3.2. National treatment is provided in regional instruments and domestic laws but with differing practices

The EAC Investment Policy enjoins Partner States to ensure regulations on non-discrimination, including on NT. As it stands, the EAC Investment Code contains a standalone two-fold provision on the principle of non-discrimination, allowing foreign investors to invest in any business activity (except those facing restrictions) and affording them NT. But this provision is broadly defined and does not provide guidance as to the components to be considered when applying such treatment. EAC countries have differing practices with respect to the principle of non-discrimination. The investment laws of Burundi, the DRC, Rwanda and South Sudan contain non-discrimination and NT provisions, though, similarly to the EAC Investment Code, they do not define such treatment concisely or refer to the criteria of "*like circumstances*". Application of NT is restricted to certain areas or regulations in some instances, such as in Burundi and DRC. Tanzania's investment law does not contain an explicit non-discrimination provision though it seemingly affords foreign and domestic investors the same guarantees. Kenya's Investment Promotion Act is silent as to the treatment afforded to foreign investors, but the minimum capital required for an investment certificate is higher for foreign investors – implying that NT is not necessarily afforded to foreign investors. Similarly, Uganda's investment law does not afford non-discriminatory treatment to foreign investors, and investors may be restricted from investing in certain activities.

While NT embodies a commitment to fairness and non-discrimination, signalling openness to foreign investment in theory, it does not guarantee the absence of discriminatory practices. Despite the intent to create a level playing field, countries may still impose restrictive regulatory measures that, in practice, hinder FDI by creating significant barriers to entry for foreign investors. Foreign investment in certain sectors may be subject to more stringent regulations and licensing requirements than applied to domestic investors, or to restrictions on foreign ownership. The FDI Index assesses the restrictiveness of such policies, considering various factors such as equity restrictions, screening mechanisms, and regulatory transparency. Even in countries with national treatment provisions, the Index may reveal instances where regulatory measures impede foreign investment, highlighting the sometimes contrasting relationship between policy intent and practical implementation.

2.3.3. Foreign ownership of land is heavily restricted in the region and leasing options vary greatly

Restrictions on foreign land ownership serve as a barrier to foreign investment by limiting access to key assets, hindering long-term planning and investment opportunities in various sectors of the economy. Land ownership regulations within the EAC commonly enforce restrictions on foreigners, often mandating leasehold tenure rather than freehold for non-citizens, with maximum lease durations varying from 25 years in the DRC to 50 years in Burundi and 99 years in Rwanda, Kenya, Uganda, and South Sudan. Leaseholds in all partner states are renewable after their expiration for up to the maximum initial lease period for both private and public agreements. In Kenya, citizens have a pre-emptive right to renew their lease unless the land is needed for public purposes, whereas non-citizens or companies with non-citizen shareholders have no pre-emptive rights. After the expiration of their land leases, it is reverted to the government and may be offered to the public competitively.

Agriculture also plays a significant role in the economy of the EAC, but foreigners often face restrictions on accessing or buying land for agricultural purposes, which may act as a barrier for attracting investments into this vital sector for economic development and food security, especially in the face of climate-related challenges. For example, the DRC's Farming Law of 2011 limits access to land only to Congolese nationals or investors whose majority is held by Congolese. Similarly, a private limited liability company incorporated in Kenya cannot, as provided in the Land Control Act of 2012, own agricultural land unless all shareholders are Kenyan citizens. In South Sudan, leaseholds for public land may be for periods of up to 30 years for agricultural investments and 60 years for forestry investment.

2.3.4. EAC mining sectors see the highest number and types of restrictions and certain countries are witnessing a surge in state equity involvement at the discretion of the government

The EAC is rich in natural resources and mining makes up a large part of its economic landscape. At the same time, it is also the most restrictive sector in the region. States sometimes use restrictive measures in the form of local or state equity participation to promote domestic ownership, enhance resource governance, and ensure that the benefits of mining activities are shared more equitably among local communities. Ensuring broader social and economic returns from mining projects is a concern of many governments worldwide. The question is whether partial state ownership is the most appropriate means to achieve this end because some concerns could potentially be addressed via more stringent tax, environmental and labour regulations. As the experience in the mining sector in Zambia has demonstrated, state ownership does not always guarantee that workers will be treated fairly or that broader benefits will be realised (Fessehaie, 2012[12]).

While not considered a restriction under the FDI Index, as partial state ownership is not discriminatory per se, foreign investors may still perceive these restrictions as limiting their control over mining operations and reducing their potential returns on investment. All EAC Partner States, except for Rwanda, mandate government participation in mining activities through equity interests. Tanzania's Mining (State Participation) Regulations set a precedent by mandating the government to maintain a minimum of 16% non-dilutable free carried interest shares in mining companies, with the potential to extend this to 50% based on tax expenditures. In the DRC, there is an automatic transfer of 10% of a company's shares to the state, a Figure that has doubled since the previous mining code in 2018. South Sudan and Uganda provide the government with an optional equity stake of up to 15% in large-scale mining operations, with Uganda retaining the right to acquire an additional 20% of shares at commercial rates. Burundi mandates the reservation of 10% of a mining company's shareholding for the state.

While some countries like Kenya, Burundi and South Sudan inaugurated compulsory state free carry shares over a decade ago, many of the region's mining laws have only incorporated state equity participation in recent years. For example, Uganda and Tanzania passed amendments establishing mandatory state equity participation in 2022 while the DRC doubled the state's free share in mining projects in 2018. The evolution of these regulations collectively reflects a trend towards increased government involvement and local participation in the mining sector across East Africa, potentially affecting foreign investment strategies and interests as further restrictions on freedom of investment are imposed.

Requirements for equity participation by a local investor are observed in some EAC countries and considered a restriction under the FDI Regulatory Restrictiveness Index. With respect to large scale mining operations in Kenya, licensees are required to list at least 20% of their equity on a local stock exchange within three years after commencement of production. In Burundi, companies must ensure the participation of Burundi nationals in the equity capital of a company in the mining sector, although the amount is not prescribed which can lead to further uncertainties.

2.3.5. Local content requirements in the mining sector may need further clarity to effectively contribute to sustainability

Many governments implement local content requirements to stimulate domestic industry and employment, particularly in extractive industries, and to ensure some long-term development impact that extends beyond the life of the project itself. But if the requirements are not tied to the ability of local firms to deliver in a timely manner while ensuring sufficient quality, they may turn out to be counterproductive by discouraging potential investors in the first place (Johnson, 2016[13]) (Sen, 2018[14]). Local content requirements are not necessarily restrictive for foreign investors, especially when they apply to the use and training of domestic workers, but they can be when applied to the purchase of local goods and services, whereby firms are required to use domestic suppliers over imports possibly contributing to higher production costs and ultimately higher prices to downstream industries and consumers (OECD, 2019[15]).

Local content requirements can have both trade and investment scopes. Those with a trade scope mandate that a specific percentage of inputs or goods be sourced from local (resident) suppliers instead of imported from abroad. Conversely, investment-focused local content requirements compel firms to source a certain proportion of their inputs or services from domestically-owned firms (as opposed to resident firms owned by domestic or foreign investors). As these measures discriminate against foreign-owned enterprises, they are considered a restriction under the FDI Index. In the EAC, many local content requirements policies discriminate based on nationality, constituting a barrier to FDI, whereas residency-based local content policies, heavily prevalent in Rwanda, are a barrier to trade and are not considered an FDI restriction under the OECD FDI Regulatory Restrictiveness Index. The consideration of local content has been increasingly emphasised in the region's policies, particularly those of the DRC, Kenya, Tanzania and Uganda, which aim to promote domestic participation and economic development in their respective industries. However, the implementation of these local content regulations faces significant challenges in several countries. In Tanzania, despite efforts to enhance local content policies in the mining sector, such measures are hindered by vague regulations, a challenging business environment, and a historical trend of deindustrialisation. Similarly, Uganda struggles with weak local capacity in its manufacturing sector, limiting its ability to effectively implement local content requirements, particularly in the emerging oil industry.

2.3.6. Discriminatory minimum threshold and paid-up capital requirements for foreign investors are common in the EAC

Minimum capital requirements often pose significant barriers to business development and growth. These requirements can significantly increase the cost of entry into a market, discouraging foreign investors from establishing or expanding operations. The higher financial thresholds may also limit the pool of potential investors willing or able to meet the criteria, reducing competition and stifling innovation in the market (World Bank, 2014[16]). In the EAC, foreign investors often need to register for an investment certificate with the state (see below). In some instances, like Rwanda, Burundi, the DRC, and Tanzania, this requirement is linked to incentives eligibility, while in others, like South Sudan, it is obligatory to establish a business that ensures economic benefit to the country.

Additionally, there are cases where the criteria for obtaining an investment licence impose higher capital requirements on foreign investors compared to domestic ones. Minimum capital requirements often fail to achieve their initial objectives of protecting consumers and creditors from risky businesses. Instead, they can hinder entrepreneurial activity and company growth, as they do not account for varying business risks and act as barriers to entry, with creditors preferring objective risk assessments over legally-imposed capital requirements (World Bank, 2014[16]). Discriminatory minimum capital requirements serve as an additional barrier for foreign investors, especially smaller and medium-sized firms. These discrepancies are particularly striking in comparison to OECD countries and larger emerging economies, with minimum capital requirements in EAC countries often five to ten times greater for foreign investors than for domestic counterparts (World Bank, 2012[17]). In Uganda, for example, foreign investors must meet a USD 250 000 threshold while domestic investors need only meet USD 50 000, whereas, in Kenya, foreign investors must meet a threshold of USD 100 000 compared to USD 10 000 for domestic investors as part of the mandatory investment certificate registration process. These thresholds necessarily discourage smaller investors who might potentially be even more likely to rely on domestic suppliers than the larger capital-intensive investors.

2.3.7. Foreign equity restrictions are also prevalent in tertiary sectors, particularly in telecommunications, financial and business services

The telecommunications sectors in Uganda and Kenya showcase differing approaches to local equity participation requirements. Uganda mandates that companies securing National Telecom Operator licences must list a minimum of 20% of their shares on the Uganda Securities Exchange within two years, emphasising regulatory efforts to bolster local involvement in the industry. Conversely, Kenya initially increased local shareholding requirements in telecommunications from 20% in 2006 to 30% by 2020, before ultimately abolishing national equity restrictions altogether to attract foreign investment and ease entry barriers. The implementation of this policy shift, announced in 2020, only materialised in August 2023, underscoring the challenges of timely legislative reform and the resulting regulatory uncertainty in the investment landscape. Similarly, engineering consulting firms in Kenya must register or incorporate locally, with at least 51% of their shareholding held by Kenyan citizens and must be registered with the Engineers Board of Kenya as per the Engineers Act, 2011. Additionally, insurance brokers in Kenya must ensure at least 60% ownership by Kenyan citizens or entities wholly owned by them, with one third of the board of directors or managing board comprising Kenyan citizens. These regulatory frameworks reflect efforts to promote local participation across various sectors, albeit with challenges in implementation and regulatory consistency.

2.4. Reflecting considerations of sustainability in the EAC Investment Code and national investment laws

The EAC Investment Code follows the design of national investment laws driven by international standards; these were initially conceived as tools through which such standards could be integrated into domestic laws and aimed at attracting investment (IISD, 2023[18]). This trend is now facing mounting backlash, as States are increasingly aware of the risk of such instruments becoming disconnected from the wider national system, and of posing legal risks and policy concerns similar to those resulting from first-generation treaties discussed above. States are therefore showing growing interest in reshaping their investment laws to address these concerns and when doing so, States should first identify the aim they seek to achieve through such laws. The design and drafting of the law will ultimately depend on its purpose and investment laws can perform different functions, varying from governing the admission and approval of new foreign investment, to administering investment or guaranteeing legal protection (IISD, 2023[18]).

In the case of the EAC, the EAC Investment Policy identifies challenges, objectives and guiding principles of investment policies:

- Challenges to inflows of FDI include lack of streamlined regulatory and legal frameworks, the non-binding nature of the EAC Investment Code and the lack of policy coherence.
- Objectives include creating an enabling environment for investment to promote and market the EAC Partner States equitably, through *inter alia* establishing a competitive investment area by enhancing clarity and policy transparency for investors and promoting the EAC as a single investment destination.
- Guiding principles include openness to both domestic and foreign investment, promotion of local content and domestic transparent and predictable regulatory framework with simplified establishment procedures, right to national, regional and international impartial arbitration, responsible and sustainable investments and maintaining the balance between the rights and obligations of investors and States in line with principles of SDGs.

When amending the EAC Investment Code, the above elements should be kept in mind. For instance, it transpires from the guiding principles of the EAC Investment Policy that any amendment to the EAC Investment Code should continue to regulate the admission of investment, the treatment afforded to investors and the dispute resolution mechanisms. The following section will analyse the EAC Investment Code of 2006 as well as national investment laws to identify sections/provisions that may be amended to better reflect the EAC Investment Policy.[7]

The EAC Investment Code, adopted in July 2006 when the EAC had only three Partner States, was conceived as a guiding tool for countries in developing their national investment laws – this means that this tool is not binding and merely facilitates the adoption of a transparent and predictable framework. All EAC Partner States have an investment law covering both domestic and foreign investors. Most of these laws were adopted or amended in the 2010s and 2020s, after the enactment of the EAC Investment Code. The laws described in this section are listed below:

- Burundi: *Law No. 1/19 of 17 June 2021 Amending Law No. 1/24 of 10 September 2008 on the Investment Code of Burundi* (2021)
- DRC: *Code des Investissements* (2002)
- Kenya: *Investment Promotion Act* (2004, amended in 2014)
- Rwanda: *Law on investment promotion and facilitation* (2021)
- South Sudan: *Investment Promotion Act* (2009)
- United Republic of Tanzania: *Tanzania Investment Act* (2022) and *Zanzibar Investment Promotion and Protection Authority Act* (2018)
- Uganda: *Investment Code Act* (2019)

Amending the EAC Investment Code and local laws is only the first step in achieving a harmonised, conducive, predictable, and transparent business environment. Subsequent enforcement of such amendments will be paramount to attain this objective and, to ensure effective implementation, EAC bodies like investment promotion agencies could play a pivotal role in overseeing Partner States' adherence to these amendments. Enforcement can be incentivised through offering support mechanisms to facilitate implementation, such as capacity buildings, technical assistance, peer-review mechanisms or implementation guides.

2.4.1. Sustainable development is rarely a central objective of investment laws, but certain elements are taken into account when applying for investment approval or incentives

Contrary to the EAC Model Investment Treaty, the EAC Investment Code contains limited language of sustainable development; its preamble merely recognises the need to pursue open, liberal and transparent investment policies that contribute to economic progress, and that such model code would enhance quantitative and qualitative foreign and local investment. Additional incentives are afforded to investments in novel and high-risk ventures as well as in undeveloped regions of Partner States. The EAC Investment Code does not prescribe any further type of commitments with respect to sustainable development.

With respect to investment laws of EAC Partner States, considerations of sustainability are addressed to varying degrees and only some of them contain general language as to sustainable investment. South Sudan's Investment Promotion Act incorporates more considerations of sustainability than other laws, to the extent that the role assigned to its investment authority is not only to encourage and promote investments that would effectively strengthen and diversify the economy, but also those that would generate employment, contribute towards the realisation of economic co-operation and integration with regional and international communities and would develop sustainable utilisation of natural resources. Notwithstanding any other provisions or rules, investments in South Sudan must observe and implement environmentally friendly corporate rules and regulations. The investment laws of the DRC and Rwanda also contain some general language of sustainable development. In the DRC, investments are defined as those designed to create or increase capacity to provide goods and services amongst others and, in order to benefit from the protection of said law, investors are required to abide by domestic regulations on the protection of environment and the conservation of nature and to train local person for technical functions. Rwanda's investment law encourages investors to invest in priority sectors of the economy and grants additional incentives to strategic investments which contribute to certain objectives, many of which relate to sustainable development. Obtaining an investment certificate is further subject to proof of technology and knowledge transfer and raw materials being sourced locally, in addition to the requirement of an environmental assessment certificate.

In other EAC investment laws, sustainability considerations often pertain to the creation of local employment, including when obtaining approvals or incentives. For instance, the investment laws of Burundi and the DRC require investment projects to adhere to laws and regulations pertaining to environmental and labour protection and offer additional advantages to specific categories of potential investors, such as women and youth or SMEs. Under Kenya's Investment Promotion Act, an investment certificate may only be granted if the proposed investment contributes to Kenya's benefit, and therefore creates jobs for Kenyans, imparts new skills and technology to the local community and facilitates technology transfer. Tanzania's Investment Act provides additional benefits to investments that generate a minimum number of local jobs or that enhance Tanzanians' know-how. Zanzibar's Investment Act emphasises the importance of local employment and, like the Tanzania Investment Act, grants additional incentives to investments employing a minimum number of locals. Uganda's Investment Code Act equally provides that the role of its investment authority is to promote and encourage investment in new technologies, skill upgrading, training and research and product development.

Some of the investment laws reviewed require the investor to undertake an environmental impact assessment or demonstrate environmental compliance of the investment. This is notably the case in Burundi, Kenya, Rwanda, South Sudan and Uganda. While some considerations of sustainable development are embedded in domestic investment laws, achieving objectives set forth in the EAC Investment Policy will require further language to that end. It would therefore be advisable to include, in the preamble of the EAC Investment Code, express language encouraging sustainable investment in the region and to elevate such a consideration into an objective.

2.4.2. Better delineation of investors' standards of protection is advisable

Except for Kenya's Investment Promotion Act – whose purpose is to promote and facilitate investments – all investment laws in the EAC provide for investors' guarantees and standards of protection. These are nevertheless broadly defined in all investment laws and, in some instances, outdated. The analysis below focuses on the non-discrimination principle, the protection against expropriation and the FET standard.

Protection against expropriation is embedded in the EAC's Investment Policy, as well as in the EAC's Model Investment Code, which protects investors against unlawful expropriation and identifies the conditions in which an expropriation may occur. No reference to indirect expropriation is made in the relevant provision. Similarly, with the exception of Kenya's Investment Promotion Act, all investment laws protect investors against unlawful expropriation, though often only succinctly. In doing so, most laws refer to their constitution. The DRC's investment law regulates expropriation more extensively than other laws examined and protects investors against both direct and indirect expropriation. Rwanda's Law on Investment Promotion and Facilitation confirms that legal rights and interests are equally protected against unlawful expropriation.

Neither the EAC Investment Policy nor the EAC Investment Model Code make any reference to FET. Similarly, except for the DRC's investment law, none of the investment laws reviewed include an FET provision. This is in line with common practice as issues of procedural fairness and government accountability are often addressed in greater details in specific domestic laws (IISD, 2023[18]). The DRC's investment law defines the FET standard by reference to principles of international law, albeit without any express positioning *vis-à-vis* such a body of rules (OECD, 2023[7]).

Hence, better delineation of substantive protections afforded to both local and foreign investors would be advisable, including in the EAC Investment Model Code. This would allow the EAC to create a more enabling yet harmonised business environment, striking the right balance between the rights and obligations of investors and the EAC Partner States, as referred to in the EAC Investment Policy.

2.4.3. Limited sustainable development related obligations for investors and investments

The EAC Investment Policy emphasises the need to maintain a balance between the rights and obligations of investors and States in line with the principles of the SDGs and to promote responsible and sustainable investments in line with the respective member states' development objectives. Most objectives outlined in the EAC Investment Policy pertain to sustainable development, to be implemented notably in the form of obligations for investors. These objectives include maximising mobilisation and utilisation of domestic capacity through encouraging its inclusion in regional and international value chains and facilitating the transfer of skills and technology.

As it presently stands, the EAC Investment Model Code does not incorporate sustainable development related obligations for investors and investments. Despite committing to pursuing investment policies that significantly contribute to the economic progress of EAC's Partner States, the code lacks effective implementation of such commitments and merely provides that information figuring in the investment certificate as defined therein (i.e. the amount or value and the description of the assets invested, the duration of the investment) amount to an obligation for the investor.

Some domestic laws, such as in Burundi, Rwanda, and the DRC include distinct chapters or sections outlining investors' obligations and others provide more ad hoc obligations. Most investment laws of the EAC Partner States include a general obligation for investors and their investments to comply with domestic legislation and regulations, as seen in Burundi, Kenya, the DRC, Tanzania, Zanzibar and Uganda. Rwanda's Investment Code is the exception, as it does not explicitly state the obligation of investors to comply with domestic law. The inclusion of such an obligation precludes investors from relying on the provision of the investment law to evade broader compliance with domestic law, bearing in mind that singling out certain types of obligations in investment laws rather than referring to general compliance with domestic laws can be questioned (IISD, 2023[18]) A limited number of investment laws impose pre-establishment obligations, such as requiring investors to provide studies on the environmental impact of the investment. This is notably the case in Burundi, Uganda and Rwanda.

Specific obligations concerning the environment are included in some of the investment laws reviewed. For instance, in Tanzania, investors are required to conduct activities in a manner that best contributes to environmental protection, creation of gender balance and skills development. In South Sudan, investors are enjoined to observe and implement environment friendly corporate rules and regulations. Labour obligations are included to a larger extent in the investment laws of the DRC, Zanzibar, Kenya and South Sudan (*e.g.* creation of local employment, contribution to skills development, contribution to technology transfer). Rwanda, Tanzania and Uganda do not impose such an obligation on investors but grant additional incentives to investors providing employment and training to locals.

Like with regional investment instruments, the degree of enforceability of these obligations is not always clear and can vary from one investment law to another. Most investment laws provide for the possibility to revoke the investment certificate, notably in the event of misrepresentation or fraudulent information when applying for the investment certificate. This is notably the case in Burundi, Kenya, Rwanda, Uganda and South Sudan. In some cases, the same penalty is also applicable for other types of breaches, such as failure to comply with the investment certificate or the relevant investment law. In Rwanda, an investor's failure to design and implement environmentally friendly rules and regulations is also punishable by fines, financial compensation or removal of the damage where applicable.

Investment laws of EAC Partner States, including more recent ones, demonstrate EAC governments' willingness to promote sustainable investment, including by imposing further sustainability-related obligations on investors. Continuing on this course and mandating investors to adhere to sustainability obligations will undoubtedly assist the EAC in attaining its objectives outlined in the EAC Investment Policy.

2.4.4. Scarce sustainable development related obligations and commitments for states

As the EAC Investment Policy endeavours to foster sustainable investment, this objective is more likely to be achieved with the active engagement and commitment of Partner States. The EAC Investment Model Code does not impose any obligation on adopting States beyond those relating to investors' substantive protection described above.

In the same vein, national investment laws in the EAC almost unanimously lack states' general obligations or commitments on key sustainable development issues. South Sudan's investment law contains some form of state obligation, to the extent that it requires the local investment authority to ensure the protection of local communities and promote indigenous investments. Uganda's investment law also requires the investment authority to comply with financial obligations, such as having regard to sound financial principles and complying with its Public Finance Management Act.

Several Partner States include other commitments in these laws which could positively contribute to sustainable development. For example, some undertake to protect intellectual property rights, and all include provisions regarding the establishment and operation of investment agencies to promote and facilitate investment. This reinforces the potential for attracting investment that could positively contribute to sustainable development.

In achieving the sustainability goals set forth in the EAC Investment Policy, EAC Partner States are encouraged to commit more solemnly to sustainability-related obligations in their investment laws, to guarantee efficient implementation and continuity of such policies in the long term.

2.4.5. Varying approaches to dispute settlement mechanisms and the availability of arbitration

The EAC Investment's Policy seeks to ensure the right to national, regional and international impartial arbitration in the event of a dispute, bearing in mind that dispute settlement should take into account new developments at varying levels.

The EAC Investment Model Code does not enjoin parties to a specific dispute settlement mechanism. Rather, parties to an investment certificate have the liberty to elect their preferred dispute settlement mechanism. Disputes to be settled by way of arbitration will, in principle, be subject to the Rules of the International Centre for the Settlement of Investment Disputes (ICSID). The inclusion of an arbitration clause in the investment certificate does not preclude the parties from resorting to any remedy including the East African Court of Justice. No mention is made as to whether prior negotiations or attempts to amicably resolve the dispute are required before resorting to contentious remedies.

Except for the investment law of Kenya, all investment laws in the EAC contain dispute settlement provisions and sometimes refer to the possible recourse to arbitration in the event of a dispute, albeit through different approaches:

- The investment law of Burundi is fairly similar to the EAC Investment Model Code in that respect, to the extent that it does not elect a dispute resolution mechanism but provides that in the event the dispute is referred to international arbitration, it shall comply with ICSID rules;
- Investment disputes arising out of the DRC's investment law shall invariably be submitted to international arbitration (ICSID or Arbitration Court of the International Chamber of Commerce of Paris);

- Investment laws of Rwanda, Tanzania, South Sudan, Zanzibar and Uganda provide for the possibility of recourse to arbitration in the event of an investment dispute. In Rwanda and Uganda, in the absence of an arbitration clause, disputes are submitted to local courts. By contrast, in Zanzibar, specific reference must be included if parties do not wish to submit their disputes to arbitration – implying that international arbitration is the default forum for resolving investment disputes. Investment laws of Tanzania and South Sudan are not clear as to the competent forum in the absence of a specific reference to that end in the investment certificate.

Prior consent to arbitration is embedded in the DRC and Zanzibar's investment laws, to the extent that no further agreement is needed to submit a dispute to arbitration. Dispute resolution provisions included in the investment laws of Tanzania and South Sudan are adversely equivocal as it remains unclear whether prior consent on behalf of the state is required to submit a dispute to arbitration, or merely necessary for the choice of applicable arbitration rules. Such provisions would benefit from clearer wording to avoid conflicting interpretations by arbitral tribunals, though they are likely to be interpreted as incorporating the States' prior consent to arbitration. In any event, providing prior consent to arbitration on behalf of a state in investment laws is uncommon and could create significant legal risks for states, associated with substantial legal costs (IISD, 2023[18]). To balance such risk, a great number of investment laws require the host government to provide its consent to arbitration separately (such as in the investment certificate). This is notably the case of the investment laws of Rwanda and Uganda, which do not provide for prior consent to arbitration on behalf of the state but rather, require that such consent be given separately in the parties' investment certificate.

Preliminary attempts at amicable settlement, before any recourse to arbitration or courts, are required in most investment laws. This is notably the case of the DRC, Rwanda, Tanzania, South Sudan, Uganda and Zanzibar. While Burundi does not include a dispute settlement provision *per se* and therefore does not include this requirement, it nevertheless enjoins its investment agency to contribute to the amicable resolution of disputes between investors and the State.

Elected arbitral institutions vary from one investment law to another, though most refer to ICSID. In addition to the possibility of arbitration under the auspices of ICSID, most investment laws allow for recourse in accordance with bilateral or multilateral agreements with the investor's home country or other agreed-upon mechanisms (*e.g.* South Sudan) or national arbitration laws (*e.g.* Uganda, Tanzania, Zanzibar).

References

AfCFTA (2023), *AfCFTA Protocol to the Agreement establishing the African Continental Free Trade Area on Investment*. [5]

EAC (2016), *EAC Model Investment Treaty*, https://edit.wti.org/document/show/pdf/062e9278-4383-4ff9-97b4-a8bbff3eb21c. [1]

Fessehaie, J. (2012), *What determines the breadth and depth of Zambia's backward linkages to copper mining? The role of public policy and value chain dynamics*, University of Cape Town PRISM, School of Economics, https://doi.org/10.1016/j.resourpol.2012.06.003. [12]

IISD (2023), *Rethinking National Investment Laws: A study of past and present laws to inform future policy-making*, https://www.iisd.org/system/files/2023-07/rethinking-national-investment-laws-en.pdf. [18]

Johnson, L. (2016), *Space for Local Content Policies and Strategies*, Columbia Law School, https://scholarship.law.columbia.edu/sustainable_investment_staffpubs/16?utm_source=scholarship.law.columbia.edu%2Fsustainable_investment_staffpubs%2F16&utm_medium=PDF&utm_campaign=PDFCoverPages. [13]

Mbengue, M. and S. Schacherer (2021), "Evolution of International Investment Agreements in Africa: Features and Challenges of Investment Law "Africanization"", in *Handbook of International Investment Law and Policy*, Springer Singapore, Singapore, https://doi.org/10.1007/978-981-13-5744-2_77-2. [9]

Mistura, F. (forthcoming), *OECD FDI Regulatory Restrictiveness Index: Methodological update*. [11]

Mistura, F. and C. Roulet (2019), "The determinants of Foreign Direct Investment: Do statutory restrictions matter?", *OECD Working Papers on International Investment*, No. 2019/01, OECD Publishing, Paris, https://doi.org/10.1787/641507ce-en. [10]

OECD (2024), *Sustainable Investment Policy Perspectives in the Economic Community of West African States (ECOWAS)*, OECD Publishing, Paris, https://doi.org/10.1787/654e2de5-en. [3]

OECD (2024), *The Future of Investment Treaties (Track 2) - About work on the Future of Investment Treaties in the Track 2 Project*, OECD, Paris, https://www.oecd.org/investment/investment-policy/oecd-future-investment-treaties-track2-faq.pdf. [2]

OECD (2023), *'Fair" and 'equitable' treatment provisions in investment treaties A large-sample survey of treaty provisions*, OECD, Paris, https://one.oecd.org/document/DAF/INV/TR1/WD(2023)1/en/pdf. [7]

OECD (2023), *Sustainable Investment Policy Perspectives in the Southern African Development Community*, OECD Publishing, Paris, https://doi.org/10.1787/02c9ef1d-en. [4]

OECD (2021), *The Future of Investment Treaties (Track 2) - The notion of 'indirect expropriation in investment treaties concluded by 88 jurisdictions: A large sample survey of treaty provisions*, OECD, Paris, https://www.oecd.org/investment/investment-policy/oecd-future-investment-treaties-indirect-expropriation-meeting-background.pdf. [6]

OECD (2019), *Local content requirements*, OECD Trade Policy Brief, February, https://issuu.com/oecd.publishing/docs/local_content_requirements. [15]

PAIC (2016), *Draft Pan-African Investment Code*. [8]

Sen, R. (2018), *Enhancing local content in Uganda's oil and gas industry.*, UNU-WIDER, https://doi.org/10.35188/UNU-WIDER/2018/552-7. [14]

U.S. Bureau of Economic Analysis (2021), *Activities of U.S. Multinational Enterprises, 2021*, https://www.bea.gov/international/di1usdop. [19]

World Bank (2014), *Why are minimum capital requirements a concern for entrepreneurs?*, World Bank Doing Busienss 2014. [16]

World Bank (2012), *Investing Across Borders database*, World Bank. [17]

Notes

[1] More information can be found at: https://www.oecd.org/en/topics/the-future-of-investment-treaties.html.

[2] The official and/or executed version of the AfCFTA Investment Protocol is not accessible online; the present analysis has therefore been conducted on the basis of the draft presented at the Seventh Extraordinary Session of the Specialized Technical Committee on Justice and Legal Affairs in Accra, Ghana, in January 2023.

[3] Note should be taken that most the EAC Partners have enacted national laws related to these topics.

[4] Pursuant to art. 46 of the AfCFTA Investment Protocol, the applicable dispute resolution is to be addressed in a separate Annex that is yet to be negotiated and published (expected within 12 months of the adoption of the protocol).

[5] Of the almost 41 000 foreign affiliates of US investors, for example, fully 92% are majority-owned and the same proportion holds for US-owned affiliates in Africa (U.S. Bureau of Economic Analysis, 2021[19]). One element which might explain this preference is the perceived need to protect intangible assets and intellectual property rights from potentially leaking to local partners and competitors.

[6] Only measures that discriminate against foreign investment in real estate for purely financial reasons — i.e. investments that are intended for leasing and capital gains, rather than support an investor's business operations — are considered restrictions under the 'real estate investment' sector. As per the OECD FDI Regulatory Restrictiveness Index methodology, even if foreign investors are allowed to lease and sub-lease real estate property, where they face discrimination in the types of land and real estate titles they can hold compared to domestic investors, a restriction on 'real estate investment' is considered to apply. Such discriminatory measures put foreign investors at a disadvantage, preventing them from equitably benefiting from all profitable investment opportunities in the market.

[7] This section looks at domestic investment laws of EAC state parties. This section does not however cover local investment legislations that go beyond investment laws, such as general tax laws, enterprise laws or commercial codes This analysis also does not cover sectoral legislation which may regulate investment in specific sectors, nor wider legislation and constitutions which may provide further details on, for instance, the rules for nationalisation and expropriation.

3 Promoting and facilitating sustainable investment

This chapter provides an overview of investment promotion agencies (IPAs) in EAC Partners States, including their organisational characteristics and main efforts to attract and facilitate sustainable investment. It also draws on the experience of other regions to provide lessons on better targeting FDI to support sustainable development and sharpening the indicators used for this purpose.

Governments design investment strategies to support national development objectives through the promotion and facilitation of foreign direct investment (FDI). Effective investment promotion strategies maximise FDI benefits by prioritising specific sectors, countries and investors and hence influencing the kind of investment that is attracted (OECD, 2018[1]). Additionally, investment facilitation measures complement these strategies to support the establishment, operations and expansions of investors that have made their location decision. This section provides an overview of the main measures taken by the EAC's Partner States in attracting and facilitating investment, particularly to support their sustainable development objectives. It looks at the strategic orientations provided in the EAC Model Investment Code (2006) and the EAC Investment Policy (2019) and offers a comparative analysis of the characteristics and priorities of individual Partner States' investment promotion agencies (IPAs).

3.1. The role of investment promotion agencies in the EAC

Most countries in the world have established IPAs to promote and facilitate investment. To support their countries' economic development efforts, IPAs are increasingly focusing on attracting more and higher-quality FDI, while also deepening the integration of their economies into global value chains (Lewis and Whyte, 2022[2]). In less advanced countries, IPAs can play a more substantial role, as international investors usually have less knowledge of local business opportunities, struggle to obtain up-to-date information and can face cultural differences (Heilbron and Kronfol, 2020[3]). In this context, all Partner States have established IPAs, which according to the EAC Investment Policy, are responsible for promoting available opportunities and facilitating investment for both local and foreign investors (Table 3.1). In the case of Tanzania, and due to its unique political structure, two investment regimes coexist, one for mainland Tanzania and one for Zanzibar, resulting in two distinct IPAs (EAC, 2019[4]).

Table 3.1. IPAs in the EAC and their establishing laws

Country	IPA name	Enabling Legislation	Year Established
Burundi	Burundi Development Agency	Law No. 1/24 of September 10, 2008, establishing the Investment Code of Burundi	2009
DRC	The National Agency for the Promotion of Investments	Decree No. 065/2002 of June 5, 2002	2002
Kenya	Kenya Investment Authority (KenInvest)	Investment Promotion Act No. 6 of 2004	2004
Rwanda	Rwanda Development Board	Organic Law n° 53/2008 of 02/09/2008	2008
South Sudan[1]	South Sudan Investment Authority	The Investment Promotion Act, 2010	2010
Uganda	Uganda Investment Authority (UIA)	The Investment Code Act, 1991	1991
Tanzania	Tanzania Investment Centre	Tanzania Investment Act, 1997	1997
Zanzibar[2]	Zanzibar Investment Promotion Authority	Zanzibar Investment Promotion and Protection Act no. 14 of 2018	2018

1. In 2020 South Sudan Investment Authority (SSIA) was transformed into the Ministry of Investment.
2. As a semi-autonomous region, Zanzibar has its own investment promotion authority.
Source: OECD compilation based on EAC IPAs' establishing statutes, 2024.

3.1.1. IPAs in the EAC are well-established and frequently involve the private sector

IPAs are established with different institutional settings, governance and strategic priorities. The way governments organise their institutional framework for investment promotion and facilitation responds to their policy objectives and the priority they give to FDI (OECD, 2020[5]). Governance structures can play a significant role in the effectiveness of IPAs' investment promotion and facilitation efforts. The EAC Model Investment Code provides that IPAs in the Partner States should be "the primary agency of the government for the purpose of coordinating, encouraging, promoting and facilitating investment in the Partner State and advising the government on the investment policy and related matters" (EAC, 2006[6]).

Except for South Sudan, where investment attraction lies within the Ministry of Investment, all EAC IPAs are constituted as semi-autonomous public agencies and were established through laws or decrees (EAC, 2019[4]). All IPAs are governed by a board of directors, which is usually formed by representatives of various governmental departments. The EAC Model Investment Code recommends Partner States to include business representatives on their IPAs' board of directors (EAC, 2006[6]). In Burundi, the DRC, Uganda, Tanzania, and Zanzibar, the boards of IPAs include at least one representative from the private sector (Figure 3.1). The Board of Directors is only chaired by private sector members in the DRC and Burundi, however, where the chair of the board is held by a representative from the private sector in the former and by the director of the chamber of commerce in the latter. Including private sector actors ensures that the interests of businesses are considered. Including other stakeholders, such as academia, trade associations and civil society, can help IPAs further enhance their accountability to investment targets and attain a better understanding of investor needs (Steenbergen, 2023[7]).

Figure 3.1. The composition of board differs across EAC IPAs

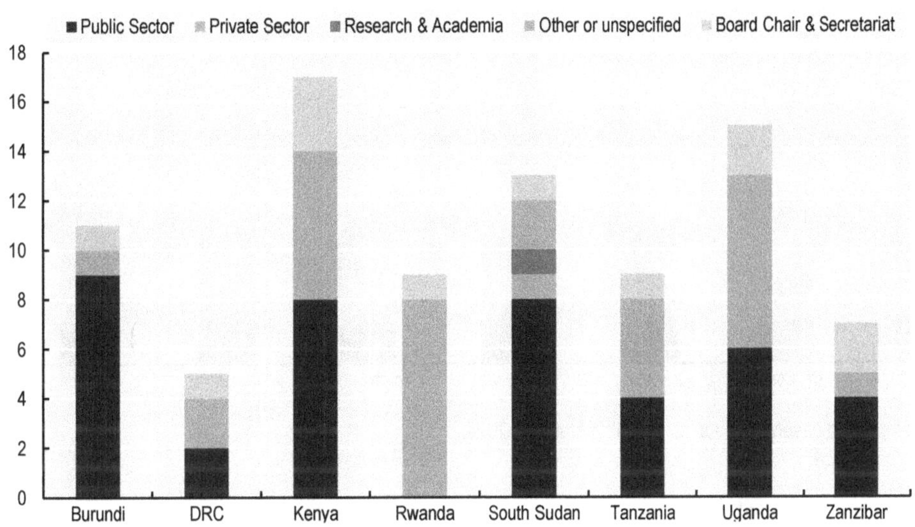

Note: The category "Board Chair & Secretariat" includes members who hold specific government-appointed roles on the board. These roles include the Chairman appointed on such terms, Director General (or Secretary General) of the IPA and Secretary of the Cabinet.
Source: OECD compilation based on IPAs' establishing statutes, 2024.

To support their activities, some IPAs have established additional offices on top of their headquarters. The Burundi Development Agency, the Kenya Investment Authority (KenInvest), the Tanzania Investment Centre, the Uganda Investment Authority and the Zanzibar Investment Promotion Authority have at least one regional office (i.e., an office in a region within their country). In the DRC, the National Agency for the Promotion of Investments, has not yet established additional offices, but its constituting law allows it to open representations or branches in other locations within the DRC or abroad by decision of the Board of Directors. The existence of regional offices can help IPAs attract FDI in these locations and support their development objectives, particularly in countries with few or no subnational agencies dedicated to investment promotion and facilitation. For instance, the regional offices of the Tanzania Investment Centre, called zonal offices, conduct investment promotion and facilitation activities at the local level by showcasing relevant investment opportunities and assisting investors in obtaining relevant permits and licences. Offices can also be located abroad. As such, the Rwanda Development Board is the only EAC IPA that has set up liaison offices in other countries, notably in Canada, China and Türkiye.

3.1.2. EAC agencies have multiple mandates and often go beyond attracting FDI

The EAC Investment Policy's overarching objective is "to create an enabling environment for investment to promote and market the EAC Partner States equitably" (EAC, 2019[4]). To achieve this objective, all EAC IPAs are mandated to promote and facilitate FDI in their respective jurisdictions, as well as to support broad economic development, such as promoting local investment, developing an attractive business environment and supporting small and medium-sized enterprises (SMEs) (Figure 3.2). In some instances, IPAs may have more specific mandates, such as export promotion (Burundi, Rwanda and Zanzibar), tourism promotion (Rwanda and Zanzibar) and the negotiation of international deals and agreements (Burundi and Rwanda). Regardless of the number of mandates, they should be coherent and well-defined, for instance, distinguishing between policymaking and implementation. Evidence shows that agencies with too many mandates that overlap or contradict those of other government agencies will struggle to deliver substantial results (Heilbron and Whyte, 2019[8]).

Figure 3.2. The scope of IPA mandates varies widely across the region

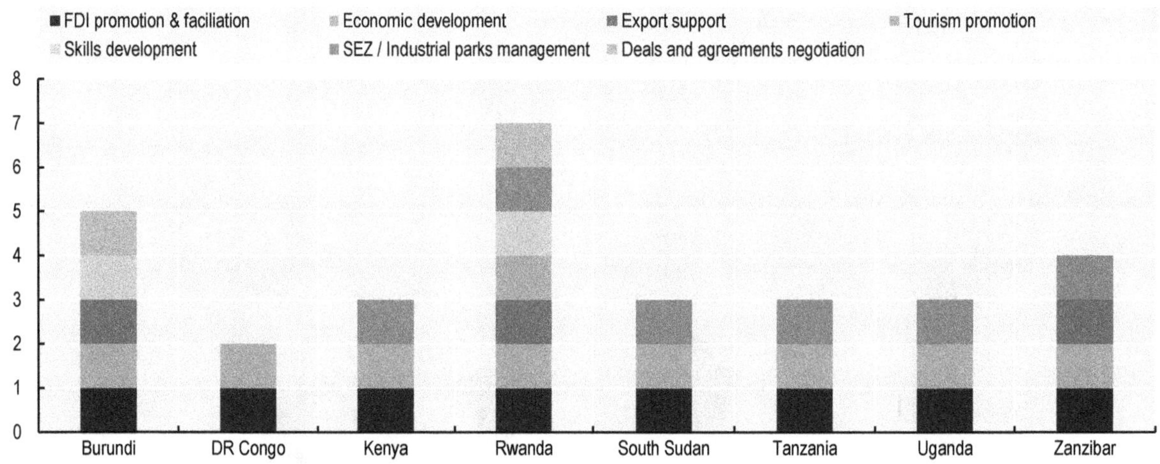

Source: OECD compilation based on IPAs' establishing statutes, 2024.

Governments may also opt to establish special economic zones (SEZs) and export processing zones (EPZs) to attract investors, create jobs and streamline procedures. These areas are often governed by a single administrative authority, which may or may not be the IPA (OECD, 2015[9]). For example, in Burundi, the Special Economic Zones Managing Authority was established to provide an enabling business environment, attract local and foreign investments, and offer fiscal and non-fiscal incentives. In other instances, the management of SEZs is directly carried out by the IPA, such as in Rwanda, South Sudan and Zanzibar. Similarly, with the upcoming merger of the Tanzania Investment Centre and the Export Processing Zone Authority, the new entity will be responsible for SEZs in addition to promoting investment. In Uganda, the IPA manages only industrial parks, as the Free Zones Act of 2014 established as a separate entity, the Uganda Free Zones Authority, which is responsible for the establishment, development, management, marketing, maintenance, supervision and control of SEZs. In Kenya, the Export Processing Zones Authority, established in 1990 by the EPZ Act, oversees the promotion and facilitation of export-oriented investments. It provides information on exporting opportunities and facilitates administrative procedures in its zones. It also advocates in favour of enhancing the ease of doing business in the country.

As the key contact point between government and investors, IPAs provide tailored services to ensure a simplified, clear and engaging experience for firms to do business within the country. A recent World Bank survey revealed that most international investors find IPA services valuable during all stages of their investment (Heilbron and Aranda-Larrey, 2020[10]). In the EAC region, all IPAs offer investment promotion and facilitation services by disseminating investment opportunities, supporting foreign investors in setting up and expanding operations, and managing grants and incentives (Figure 3.3). To ensure that services are delivered in an efficient and transparent manners, IPAs can provide client charters to set targets for service delivery and detailing the expected timeline, costs and requirements associated to each service. While KenInvest, publishes comprehensive client charters covering all these aspects, the Rwanda Development Board provides information on service timescales but not on costs or requirements. Other EAC IPAs lack such detailed client charters, resulting in potential lower levels of investor confidence. Timestamped client charters could ensure that investors are updated on current IPA practices and standards in the support services offered. Additionally, most IPAs also provide information on legal and administrative procedures and engage in policy advocacy with relevant authorities. Compared to IPAs from other regions in the continent, namely ECOWAS and SADC, EAC IPAs tend to engage more in policy advocacy, while fewer organise matchmaking and networking events and provide strategic business advice (i.e., marketing, financial or administrative support when entering their home market).

Figure 3.3. EAC IPAs offer a wide range of services to investors

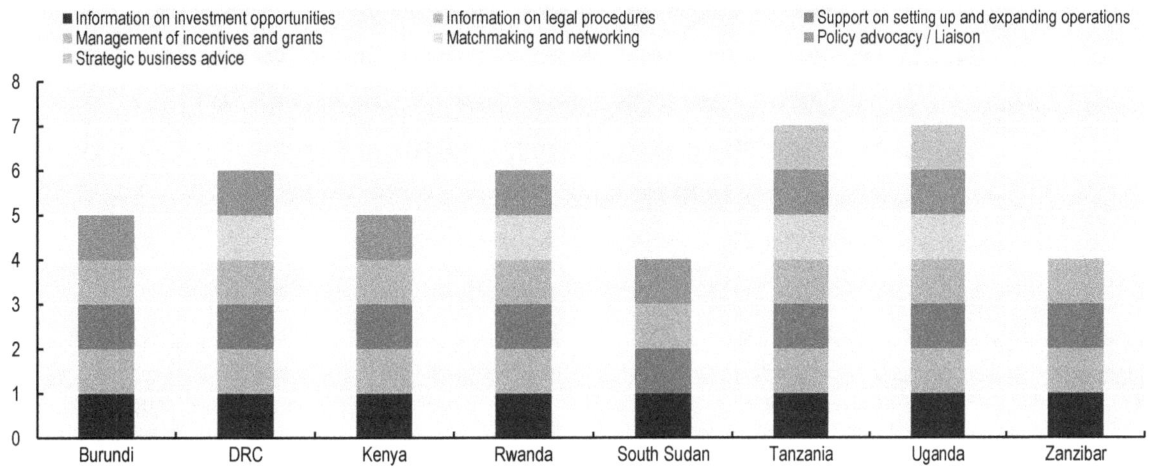

Source: OECD compilation based on IPAs' websites, 2024.

3.1.3. IPAs are progressively leveraging digitalisation to facilitate investment

One-stop-shops (OSSs) are one of the primary tools at the disposal of governments to facilitate investment. If well-designed, they can be a deciding factor for investors when selecting an investment destination as they tend to cut down transaction costs by streamlining administrative procedures, reducing information asymmetries and providing clarity on current investment policies (OECD, 2015[9]). OSSs can be of different types: they range from entry points for investors, providing relevant information on administrative requirements (such as in Burundi, the DRC and South Sudan) to fully-fledged platforms, centralising under the same roof all or most necessary procedures to invest (such as in Kenya, Rwanda, Tanzania, Uganda and Zanzibar).

The EAC Model Investment Code stipulates that all IPAs shall operate an OSS and assist investors in matters related to fiscal requirements, investment registration forms, environmental impact assessments, entry and visa permits, and the procurement of land and utilities (EAC, 2006[6]). Except for South Sudan, all agencies in the region provide information on business creation and registration, with most of them also sharing information on taxation and exemptions, and investment certificates (Figure 3.4). When relevant, IPAs also offer information on the general costs and fees charged as well as on the licences required to operate in regulated sectors, such as mining, banking and healthcare. But more comprehensive client charters indicating the expected time and costs of each procedure could be established to increase transparency and investor confidence. These procedures are also not always supported by the Partner States' OSSs – particularly those that act just as mere information providers – and therefore must be completed through the corresponding department or ministry. If investors have to independently contact too many authorities separately, the effectiveness and usefulness of OSSs diminishes significantly. Whole-of-government approaches in investment facilitation (including through the OSSs) could streamline processes and reduce redundancy, preventing investors from having to navigate multiple departments, through interagency co-ordination and integrated information systems for data sharing and communication.

Figure 3.4. OSSs in the EAC provide relevant information to investors but centralise less systematically the necessary procedures

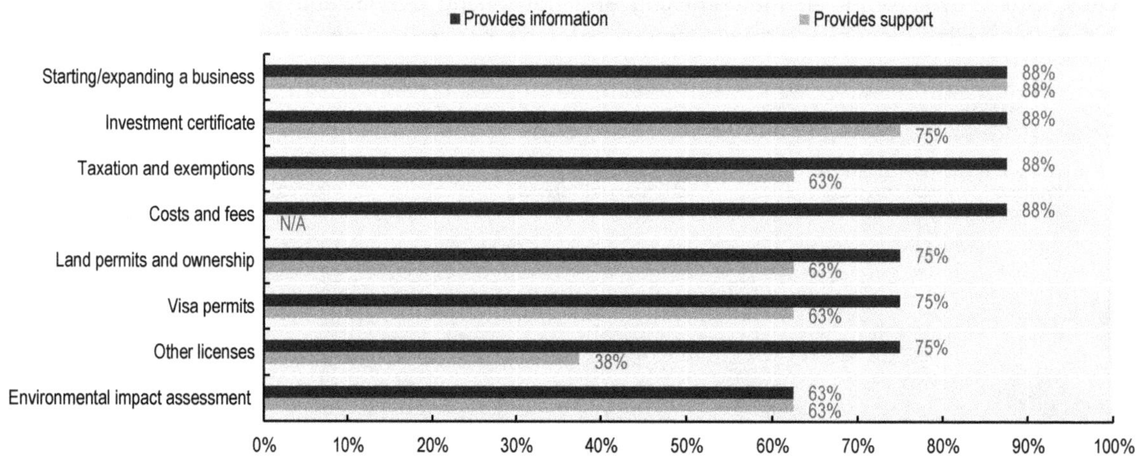

Note: "Provides information" refers to the cases where the OSS portal provides information on the steps to follow, the documentation required and the relevant authority to contact. "Provides support" refers to the cases where the OSS directly supports investors in completing the necessary procedures. The percentages represent the total number of IPAs; thus, Tanzania and Zanzibar are counted separately.
Source: OECD compilation based on IPAs' and OSSs' websites, 2024.

To offer simplified, streamlined and centralised investment-related procedures, IPAs could further embrace the digital transformation, improving transparency, promoting effective communication and reducing barriers to entry. In the OECD, half of IPAs have migrated most of their procedures to an online platform, with over 30% of them having fully digitalised the process to start a business and invest (de Crombrugghe and Moore, 2021[11]). Understanding the importance of digitalisation, Partner States have started adopting digital tools to improve their investment facilitation activities. For instance, in 2015, KenInvest began using the eRegulations online platform, providing a detailed, step-by-step description of administrative procedures, as well as associated costs, legal justifications and contact details of relevant officials. As a result, KenInvest has seen a rise in positive feedback from prospective investors and has managed to improve collaboration efforts with partner governmental agencies (UNCTAD, 2017[12]).

Rwanda's One Stop Centre has been at the forefront of the country's investment facilitation efforts, offering one of the fastest business registration processes in Africa (US Department of State, 2023[13]). Besides providing information and support on basic procedures related to the establishment of operations, the agency also shares relevant information on consumer protection, tourism regulation and workforce availability. Furthermore, most of these procedures can be completed online, without the physical presence of the investors being required in the respective agencies or ministries. This has resulted in Rwanda being frequently ranked among the best countries for doing business in Africa. On its Doing Business indicator (2020), the World Bank ranked it the second-best country in Africa, just after Mauritius, and the first among EAC Partner States, leading in the categories related to starting a business, dealing with construction permits and registering property (World Bank, 2020[14]).

OSSs need to be well-established to function efficiently and avoid unnecessary transactional costs; Egypt and the United Kingdom provide good practice examples (Box 3.1). To complement well-functioning OOSs, initiatives can also be developed at the regional level. For example, it could be envisaged to establish an investors' helpdesk at the EAC Secretariat to support prospective investors interested in the region.

Box 3.1. Good practices on One-Stop-Shops

One-stop-shops can significantly reduce transaction costs for businesses and facilitate the establishment of foreign firms in the country. Nevertheless, they run the risk of becoming "one-more stop" if officials do not have sufficient decision-making powers and full approval authority, leading to a duplication of responsibilities and increased uncertainty for foreign investors.

Investors Services Centres (ISCs) – Egypt

With the promulgation of the 2017 Investment Law and as part of Egypt's investment climate reforms, ISCs were created to grant approvals, certifications and licences necessary for establishing and operating a company in the country. These one-stop-shops provide full start-to-end services to investors, including those related to establishing companies and their branches, approving the minutes of their boards of directors and their general assemblies, issuing approvals and permits, and allocating the necessary real estate for the establishment of projects. ISCs also leverage digital tools to streamline business registration procedures, such as the electronic signature service that enables reducing the time needed for certain procedures. The ISCs follow a number of good international practices. For instance, they are not mandatory entry points for investors, which incentivises them to remain efficient. ISCs are also equipped with a customer relationship management (CRM) system, which includes key performance indicators for monitoring performance. As a result, ISCs have been welcomed by the international business community in Egypt.

GOV.UK – United Kingdom

As part of its digital strategy, the United Kingdom's government launched in 2010 the single online domain "GOV.UK" to provide a consistent user experience with access to joined-up government services. The website is the starting point for more than 150 government procedures, providing information, guidance and services for businesses and citizens (both local and foreign) on company registration, taxation, visa procedures, exports of goods, among others. While the site is maintained by the Government Digital Service (GDS), individual departments and agencies are still responsible for drafting and managing their own information and services. The GDS includes important features to continuously improve the platform, for instance, they developed a "step-by-step" navigation feature that allows any service to be represented as a series of simple steps. Furthermore, feedback buttons have been integrated on every page so users can provide critical feedback on their experience and report their level of satisfaction when using the available information and services.

Source: (OECD, 2020[5]; OECD, 2020[15]).

3.2. Attracting FDI in support of sustainable development

3.2.1. Partner States promote a range of diversified sectors…

With rising international competition for FDI, IPAs increasingly seek to prioritise certain sectors over others, as it allows them to target investments that are potentially more beneficial for their economy and better align with national development plans. By focusing on a select number of priority sectors rather than attending to all types of investors, IPAs can improve the effectiveness of their FDI attraction efforts

(Sztajerowska and Volpe Martincus, 2021[16]). While priority sectors differ between Partner States, all focus on promoting agricultural and tourism related investments. For the agricultural sector, they highlight opportunities on crops intended to produce edible oils (e.g., soybean, sunflower, palm) and horticulture (e.g., fruits, vegetables, ornamental plants). Partner States also prioritise investments in manufacturing, mining, information and communications technology (ICT), and energy, focusing particularly on sustainable investment projects in the latter (see below). Other specific sectors that EAC IPAs also promote include forestry (the DRC and South Sudan) and services (Rwanda). Compared to IPAs in the ECOWAS and SADC regions, EAC IPAs focus more on health, fishing and the financial sector, but prioritise less the transport and textile sectors (Table 3.2).

Table 3.2. Priority sectors for investment promotion in EAC Partner States

Sector	BDI	COD	KEN	RWA	SSD	TZA	UGA	EAC	ECOWAS	SADC
Agriculture	■	■	■	■	■	■	■	100%	100%	100%
Communication (ICT)	■	■	■	■		■	■	86%	80%	81%
Education	■			■				29%	13%	38%
Energy	■	■		■	■	■	■	86%	80%	88%
Finance & Insurance	■	■	■	■		■		71%	27%	50%
Fishing	■	■	■		■	■		71%	53%	38%
Health	■		■	■		■	■	71%	27%	44%
Manufacturing	■	■	■	■		■	■	86%	67%	69%
Infrastructure & Real Estate		■	■	■		■	■	71%	73%	63%
Livestock		■	■		■	■		57%	47%	N/A
Mining	■	■		■	■	■	■	86%	60%	69%
Textile			■			■		29%	40%	N/A
Tourism	■	■	■	■	■	■	■	100%	73%	94%
Transportation & Logistics		■						14%	47%	31%

Note: Coloured cells represent the sectors that are promoted.
Source: OECD compilation based on IPAs' websites, 2024.

The EAC Investment Policy also highlights a list of sectors that offer attractive investment opportunities. It emphasises agriculture, infrastructure and real estate, manufacturing, tourism and services (including finance, health and education) as targeted sectors for foreign investors. In the energy sector, it highlights opportunities in mining, oil and gas, but also in renewable energy sources, such as biomass, hydropower, geothermal, solar and wind (EAC, 2019[4]).

3.2.2. … and progressively prioritise sustainable industries

Governments can harness FDI to meet the SDGs. To achieve this, they should not only focus on the volume of investment projects attracted, but also on their capacity to positively affect the diverse angles of sustainable development (Sauvant and Mann, 2019[17]). All agencies in the region put a special emphasis on promoting sustainable FDI. In particular, renewable energies are very actively promoted by EAC IPAs, as 86% of them seek to attract investments in this sector, notably for solar, wind and hydropower projects (Table 3.3). In comparison, in ECOWAS and SADC, only 67% and 63% of member countries prioritise renewable energies, respectively. While KenInvest does not actively target FDI projects in the energy sector, Kenya still enjoys a leading position in clean energy development, with more than 90% of the country's on-grid electricity originating from renewable sources (US Department of State, 2023[18]).

Table 3.3. Prioritisation of renewable energies in EAC Partner States

Country	BDI	COD	KEN	RWA	SSD	TZA	UGA
Energy type	Geothermal Hydropower Solar Wind	Biomass Hydropower Natural gas Solar Wind	*No active targeting*	Biomass Hydropower Solar	Hydropower Solar	Biomass Geothermal Hydropower Natural gas Nuclear Solar Wind	Geothermal Hydropower Solar

Source: OECD compilation based on IPAs' websites, 2024.

Other sustainable investments promoted include reforestation, sustainable agriculture and eco-tourism. For example, the National Investment Promotion Agency of the DRC seeks to attract investments to plant around three million hectares of forest by 2025 with the objective of removing three million tons of CO_2 equivalent and generating more than 30 000 jobs. KenInvest works towards ensuring food security by promoting investments that make use of organic farming methods and embrace technological advances to enhance climate change resilience. The Rwanda Development Board offers investment opportunities in conservation projects and natural parks, such as the Volcanoes National Park Experiential Centre and the Kigali Cultural Village, as a means of conserving the country's natural heritage while also diversifying tourism income and expanding research-oriented activities.

Several IPAs have taken additional steps to advance sustainable investment. KenInvest's 2023-2027 Strategic Plan, entitled "Spearheading Equitable Investment-Led Transformation," includes strategic responses aimed at targeting different SDGs as part of its economic recovery strategies. The latter are designed to reposition the economy for steady, inclusive, and sustainable growth. Additionally, the Rwanda Development Board entered into a joint venture with a private company in 2019 for the development of the Gabiro Agribusiness Hub Project, a holistic and commercial agricultural ecosystem. By 2024, this initiative has attracted seven companies involved in the production of high-value crops aimed at enhancing food security, specifically targeting SDG 2 (Zero Hunger). The SDG Investments Tanzania Platform of the Tanzania Investment Centre provides another illustration. Developed in co-operation with the United Nations Development Programme, its goal is to mobilise sustainable investment by providing information on business opportunities with the potential to contribute to sustainable development. Zanzibar launched its Blue Economy Policy in 2020, which seeks to reap the economic benefits of marine and coastal resources to support economic growth, employment generation and investment attraction, without jeopardising the ecosystem. It targets the sectors of fisheries, maritime trade, energy and tourism.

3.2.3. Investment tracking is centred around simple assessment metrics

Beyond targeting investments in sustainable sectors, IPAs should track their contribution in attracting FDI and measuring its impact on sustainable development. Effective assessment can provide IPAs with vital information on the effects that foreign-owned firms have on job-creation, environmental protection and innovation generation (OECD, 2019[19]). To achieve this, EAC IPAs could capitalise on the SDGs as a basis for their prioritisation and monitoring and evaluation efforts. The Republic of Türkiye's Investment Office provides a concrete example on how IPAs can draw upon the SDGs to adopt a scoring mechanism aiming at prioritising both incoming and current investment projects by weighing their contribution to the SDGs (Box 3.2).

Box 3.2. Türkiye's sustainable investment scoring mechanism

In line with the national strategy of promoting quality FDI, the Investment Office of the Presidency of the Republic of Türkiye launched a new scoring mechanism, which prioritises investment projects based on five pillars: investment size, direct contributions, potential contributions, investor prestige and SDG compliance. For the last pillar, the IPA developed a survey made up of a series of simple questions on whether investors comply with specific SDGs through their investment project. The table below provides an illustration:

Table 3.4. SDG 4. Quality Education

Questions	Yes (5) / No (0)	Weight
1. Does the investment to be made by the company include a technical training center or R&D, design, innovation center investment?		20%
2. Is it an investment that is open to university - industry cooperation and has the potential to cooperate with technical education and vocational high schools and research institutes?		20%
3. Is it possible to provide technical training at home or abroad for the personnel to be employed within the investment?		20%
4. Is it an investment with the potential to deliver technology/knowledge spillovers to other stakeholders in the ecosystem?		20%
5. Is it an investment that creates intense employment in the fields of STEM (Science, Technology, Engineering and Math)?		20%

Based on the results of the questionnaire, the Investment Office then categorises investment projects, with higher priority given to those that score higher on sustainability vis-à-vis the other pillars. To ensure effective prioritisation and that the investment project aligns with sustainability objectives, the scoring mechanism is used for both ex-ante and ex-post analysis. The agency scores the investment project before the investor makes its location decision (potential investments), once the location has been decided (attracted investments) and after the project has been established (realised investments). As such, the scoring mechanism is also used as an impact assessment tool, supporting the Investment Office's monitoring and evaluation efforts.

Source: Presentation delivered by the Investment Office of the Presidency of the Republic of Türkiye.

To use FDI to support the implementation of the SDGs, Partner States need to ensure that the indicators used by their IPAs to prioritise investments and to measure their outcomes are aligned with their overarching investment promotion strategies. IPAs need to rely on specific and consistent indicators – which must go beyond metrics relating to the number and value of investment projects or on the number of jobs created – to ensure that they attract the right investments and that the attracted FDI generates the desired outcomes. Some EAC IPAs have already begun developing holistic monitoring and evaluation frameworks. For instance, as part of KenInvest's Strategic Plan: 2023-2027, an annual investment survey must be conducted to determine whether investment targets are contributing to Kenya's Vision 2030 (i.e., Kenya's national development plan). It includes specific strategic objectives and their respective outcome indicators, some of which address different aspects of sustainability.

References

de Crombrugghe, A. and S. Moore (2021), *Investment Promotion and the Digital Economy: a Comparative Analysis of Investment Promotion Practices Across the OECD*, https://www.oecd.org/daf/inv/investment-policy/Investment-Insights-Investment-Promotion-Digital-Economy-OECD.pdf. [11]

EAC (2019), *East African Community Investment Policy*. [4]

EAC (2006), *The East African Model Investment Code*. [6]

Heilbron, A. and Y. Aranda-Larrey (2020), *Strengthening Service Delivery of Investment Promotion Agencies*, https://documents1.worldbank.org/curated/en/375281584479055974/pdf/Strengthening-Service-Delivery-of-Investment-Promotion-Agencies-The-Comprehensive-Investor-Services-Framework.pdf. [10]

Heilbron, A. and H. Kronfol (2020), *Increasing the Development Impact of Investment Promotion Agencies*, https://doi.org/10.1596/978-1-4648-1536-2_ch5. [3]

Heilbron, A. and R. Whyte (2019), *Institutions for Investment: Establishing a High-Performing Institutional Framework for Foreign Direct Investment*, https://openknowledge.worldbank.org/server/api/core/bitstreams/5c6f8f40-d564-597b-a319-72f428de2e04/content. [8]

Lewis, P. and R. Whyte (2022), *The Role of Subnational Investment Promotion Agencies*, https://documents1.worldbank.org/curated/en/099245210012218194/pdf/P17553808bd2a306a090420a272cf45ddc6.pdf. [2]

OECD (2020), *OECD Investment Policy Reviews: Egypt 2020*, OECD Publishing, Paris, https://doi.org/10.1787/9f9c589a-en. [5]

OECD (2020), *One-Stop Shops for Citizens and Business*, OECD Best Practice Principles for Regulatory Policy, OECD Publishing, Paris, https://doi.org/10.1787/b0b0924e-en. [15]

OECD (2019), "Monitoring and Evaluation: A Brief Guide for Investment Promotion Agencies", *OECD Business and Finance Policy Papers*, No. 50, OECD Publishing, Paris, https://doi.org/10.1787/82d55c1a-en. [19]

OECD (2018), *Mapping of Investment Promotion Agencies in OECD countries*, OECD, Paris, https://www.oecd.org/investment/investment-policy/mapping-of-investment-promotion-agencies-in-OECD-countries.pdf. [1]

OECD (2015), *Policy Framework for Investment*, OECD Publishing, Paris, https://doi.org/10.1787/9789264208667-en. [9]

Sauvant, K. and H. Mann (2019), *Towards an Indicative List of FDI Sustainability Characteristics*, https://ssrn.com/abstract=3055961. [17]

Steenbergen, V. (2023), *What Makes an Investment Promotion Agency Effective? Findings from a Structural Gravity Model*, The World Bank, https://doi.org/10.1596/1813-9450-10276. [7]

Sztajerowska, M. and C. Volpe Martincus (2021), *Together or Apart: Investment Promotion Agencies' Prioritisation and Monitoring and Evaluation Strategies for Sustainable Investment Promotion Across the OECD Countries*, OECD, Paris, https://www.oecd.org/daf/inv/investment-policy/Investment-Insights-Investment-Promotion-Prioritisation-OECD.pdf. [16]

UNCTAD (2017), *Investment Facilitation: The Perfect Match for Investment Promotion*, https://unctad.org/system/files/official-document/webdiaepcb2017d4_en.pdf. [12]

US Department of State (2023), *2023 Investment Climate Statements: Kenya*, https://www.state.gov/reports/2023-investment-climate-statements/kenya/. [18]

US Department of State (2023), *2023 Investment Climate Statements: Rwanda*, https://www.state.gov/reports/2023-investment-climate-statements/rwanda/. [13]

World Bank (2020), *Doing Business 2020: Economy Profile Rwanda*, https://www.doingbusiness.org/content/dam/doingBusiness/country/r/rwanda/RWA.pdf. [14]

4 Assessing the use and design of investment tax incentives

This chapter focuses on the design and policy goals of corporate income tax (CIT) incentives in the EAC Partner States and compares them to other regions. The analysis is based on comparable data from the OECD Investment Tax Incentive Database, covering CIT incentives across 65 developing and emerging countries

4.1. Incentives strategies should not neglect their potential fiscal costs

When designing incentives, striking the right balance between fostering an attractive investment environment and protecting public finances can be challenging (OECD, 2022[1]). In addition to the country context, macro-economic and legal framework conditions, design features of tax incentives play a key role in determining their success. Regional co-operation of EAC countries on tax incentives provides opportunities to align strategic priorities and strengthen the investment climate. Article 80 of the Treaty establishing the EAC prioritises the harmonisation and rationalisation of investment initiatives towards promoting the Community as a single investment destination (EAC, 2000[2]). The EAC Investment Policy outlines incentive opportunities in the region, identifies challenges for incentive up-take and pleads for establishing a monitoring and evaluation framework (EAC, 2019[3]).

This chapter focuses on the design of corporate income tax (CIT) incentives in the seven EAC countries under review and compares to the peer regions ECOWAS and SADC.[1] The analysis is based on comparable CIT data from the OECD Investment Tax Incentive Database (ITID), covering CIT incentives across 65 developing and emerging economies, including the seven EAC countries covered in this report. Granular and comprehensive data are indispensable to improve our understanding of existing tax incentive policies and to enhance the analysis of their impacts, given that their effectiveness and costs are strongly design- and context-specific. Analysis of incentive design can inform assessments of whether incentives support positive economic, social and environmental spillovers, and at what costs. For more information on methodology, scope and key classifications of the OECD ITID (see Celani, Dressler and Wermelinger (2022[4])).

EAC Partners States and many countries around the world consider tax incentives as a key tool of their investment promotion strategies. While tax incentives are commonly used, their benefits and costs are often not well understood. They have the potential to attract investment, can help to correct market failures and encourage positive spillover effects of FDI. The extent to which tax incentives can influence investment decisions depends on many factors, including the country-context and the investor and project sensitivity to incentives. In most surveys, investors consider incentives as one, but not the most important, factor for their investment decision, as incentives cannot compensate for other more fundamental shortcomings in the investment climate, such as regulatory uncertainty, burdensome administrative procedures and institutional or political instability (UNIDO, 2013[5]; IMF/OECD, 2017[6]; UN/CIAT, 2018[7]). If countries decide to offer incentives, they should use them to complement, rather than replace initiatives to improve the investment climate. Tax incentives can cause distortions and involve significant costs in terms of revenues forgone, limiting a state's resources for advancing needed reforms and public investment, including improving the business environment.

Tax revenues in the EAC are lower than in peer regions, amounting to 13% of GDP compared to 14% in ECOWAS and 18% in SADC in 2021 (Figure 4.1). CIT revenues are particularly low in Kenya, Tanzania and Uganda, ranging from 1.1% to 1.6% of GDP, below the regional average of EAC, ECOWAS and SADC, but reach 3.5% in Rwanda. Low CIT revenues can result from weaknesses in tax policy design – including offering incentives that narrow the tax base – and tax administration, such as burdensome administrative procedures and ineffective enforcement, often linked to low institutional capacity. Some EAC countries have undertaken substantive reforms to enhance their tax environment in recent years. All Partner States, except the DRC, are members of the African Tax Administration Forum, which aims to improve tax systems in Africa through exchanges, knowledge dissemination and capacity development (e.g., through courses and training programmes). For instance, South Sudan recently joined a technical assistance programme to enhance its tax dispute resolution framework (ATAF, 2023[8]).

Figure 4.1. Tax revenues have been low in the EAC

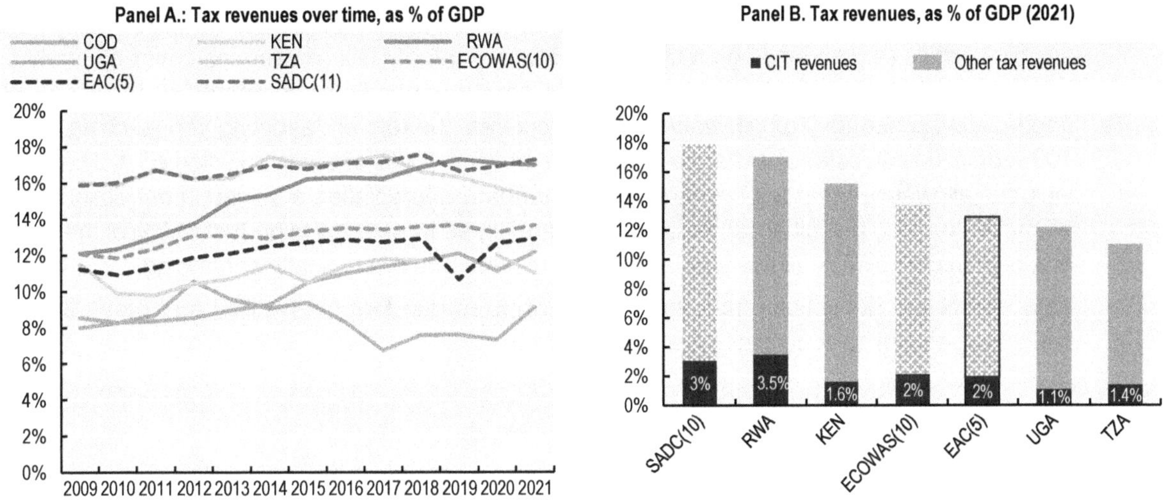

Note: Tax revenue data was only available for some countries.
Source: Authors calculations based on OECD (2023[9]), OECD Global revenue statistics (database), https://stats.oecd.org/Index.aspx?DataSetCode=RS_GBL

4.2. Strengthening tax incentive design in the EAC

Design features relate to how the incentive reduces taxation, such as the instrument used (the qualifying income or expenditure it applies to, the generosity, and duration; see Box 4.1), the eligibility conditions (defining which investors and projects qualify for the incentive), and the governance structure (detailing how the incentive is awarded to investors) (Celani, Dressler and Wermelinger, 2022[4]). These elements determine which investors can benefit, whether incentives promote certain policy goals, what are their potential costs and whether they can influence investor behaviour (OECD, 2022[1]; James, 2014[10]; IMF et al., 2015[11]). The OECD ITID offers insights into the use of CIT incentives in seven EAC Partner States, how their design features support certain policy goals and allows to compare with practices of other regional groups, notably ECOWAS and SADC. The analysis in this section complements other sections of the review, including those covering the role of investment promotion agencies and the attraction of FDI in specific sectors.

Box 4.1. Common tax incentive instruments

Investment tax incentives provide favourable deviations from the standard tax treatment for a specific group of corporate taxpayers, based on sector, activity, location or other investor- or project-related characteristics. The most commonly observed CIT incentives are often categorised as **income-based tax incentives** (CIT exemptions and reduced CIT rates), which relate to the income generated by a firm, and **expenditure-based tax incentives** (tax allowances and tax credits), which relate to firm's capital or current expenditure.

- **Tax exemptions** provide a full (100%) or partial (less than 100%) exemption of qualifying taxable income, which may refer to all of a business' income or income from particular sources (e.g. export income).
- **Reduced rates** are CIT rates set below the standard rate for qualifying taxable income and apply on a temporary or permanent basis.

- **Tax allowances** are deductions from taxable income (i.e. income subject to taxes) and may target current or capital expenditures. Qualifying capital expenditures are generally asset specific (e.g., machinery, buildings, equipment). Qualifying current expenditures tend to be activity specific (e.g., spending on training, R&D, exporting). Tax allowances cover a variety of instruments that allow for a faster write-off of capital expenditure compared to the standard depreciation schedule. Tax allowances can *accelerate* the rate of deducting capital costs (up to 100% of incurred costs) or *enhance* deductions beyond 100% of the acquisition cost. The latter includes allowances that apply in addition to standard depreciation resulting in deductions that effectively exceed the initial capital cost, for example, allowing firms to deduct 150% of the value of a new machine. Tax allowances for current expenditure are typically enhancing.
- **Tax credits** are deductions from the amount of taxes due (i.e. tax liability) that may relate to capital expenditures or current expenditures.

Source: Celani, Dressler and Wermelinger (2022[4]), https://doi.org/10.1787/62e075a9-en; and Celani, Dressler and Hanappi (2022[12]), https://doi.org/10.1787/22235558.

4.2.1. Tax exemptions and reduced rates prevail but expenditure-based incentives are rising

Income-based incentives (CIT exemptions and reduced CIT rates) are commonly used in developing and emerging economies and represent key incentives, featuring prominently in investment promotional material, in all examined EAC countries, except South Sudan. In addition to potentially involving significant costs in terms of revenues forgone and economic distortions, it is not clear to which extent incentives effectively attract *additional* investment (IMF et al., 2015[11]). Income-based incentives disproportionately favour projects that are already profitable in the early stage of operation, which can create a bias towards mobile foreign investment and risks generating windfall gains for projects likely to be least in need of additional support (Klemm and Van Parys, 2012[13]; James, 2014[10]).

Many countries seem to feel pressured to offer generous CIT exemptions and reduced rates due to global competition. Between 77-100% of countries in peer regions offer CIT exemptions, compared to 86% in the EAC (Figure 4.2, Panel A). Except South Sudan, EAC countries use income-based incentives more often than other tax instruments, offering each at least two CIT incentives that take the form of CIT exemptions or reduced CIT rates (Figure 4.2, Panel B). Most income-based incentives granted in the EAC are temporary, in line with good practice. Exemptions are particularly costly as they typically provide multiple years of full tax relief. Investors can benefit from ten-year exemptions in Burundi, Kenya, Tanzania and Uganda, and up to five and seven years in the DRC and Rwanda, respectively.

Over half of EAC countries (or 57%) offer reduced CIT rates to investors, more than ECOWAS (43%) but a lower share compared to SADC (85%) (Figure 4.2, Panel A). Most countries offer reduce rates temporarily, ranging from three to ten years, granting partial tax relief to investors. Rwanda is the only EAC country offering a zero-rate (for headquarters in Rwanda, with a five-year duration but with an option for renewal). Three countries (Burundi, the DRC, and Kenya) combine both instruments for some of their incentives, providing exemptions that are followed by reduced rates. For instance, Kenya provides a ten-year reduced rate for export processing zone enterprises, followed by a ten-year reduced rate of 25%. In Burundi, free zone companies can benefit from a ten-year tax exemption followed by a permanently reduced rate of 10%. Stability is important to investors, but when incentive recipients gain permanent preferential treatment vis-à-vis competitors, incentives can become a tool for rent-seeking (Abramovsky et al., 2018[14]).

Figure 4.2. Tax allowances are rising but most incentives use income-based instruments

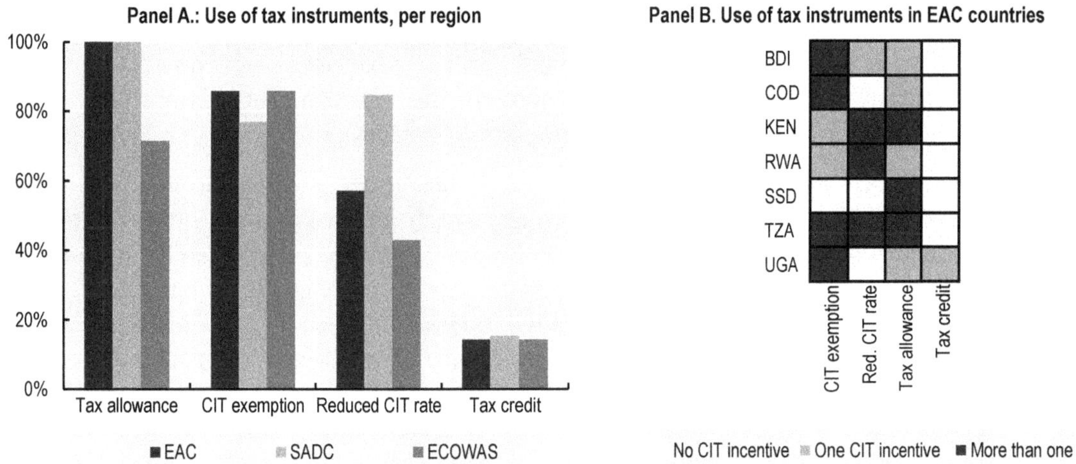

Note: Panel A.: as % of countries per region, using the indicated tax instrument for at least one CIT incentive; Panel B: Number of CIT incentives using the indicated tax instrument, per EAC country
Source: OECD ITID, February 2024, based on 65 economies and 707 CIT incentive entries.

Sunset clauses are a positive design feature, that is not yet used by EAC countries. Stipulating in the incentive-introducing provision that the measure will only be available until a certain date can facilitate revisions and phase-out of a measure for policy makers, for example, if an incentive appears to be too costly or not reaching its policy goal. Time-bound incentives may also encourage investors to undertake investments immediately, as the incentive is only available for a certain period (Celani, Dressler and Wermelinger, 2022[4]). When revising their incentives, EAC Partner States are recommended to consider using sunset clauses.

CIT exemptions and reduced CIT rates are particularly affected by the global minimum tax. The new international agreement establishing the global minimum tax (GMT) for large multinational enterprises (MNEs) could curb harmful tax competition and encourage better incentive design. The DRC and Kenya are two out of 140 participating jurisdictions. Even if the other EAC countries do not participate in the agreement, they can be affected if home jurisdictions of foreign investors are treaty parties. The agreement requires MNEs with revenues above USD 750 million to pay a 15% minimum effective tax rate (ETR) in all jurisdictions in which they operate. If affiliates of an in-scope MNE in a participating or non-participating EAC country are subject to an ETR below 15% (for example, because a reduced CIT rate or exemption applies), top-up taxes may be due. In the absence of tax reform or other policy actions, EAC countries could potentially forgo revenues arising from low-taxed profit in their jurisdiction that would be collected by other jurisdictions. It is thus advisable that countries having generous incentives packages, such as EAC Partner States, consider the implications of the minimum tax on their tax incentives and investors.

While income-based incentives prevail, expenditure-based instruments (tax allowances and credits) are rising. All EAC countries offer at least one tax allowance to investors, which is in line with practices observed in SADC but higher than those applied in ECOWAS. Most allowances relate to capital assets, notably buildings, machinery and equipment, and accelerate cost-recovery, most of them in the form of initial allowances that provide a higher depreciation rate in the year of investment. Kenya also offers enhancing allowances of up to 150% of expenditure occurred for capital assets used for manufacturing. Uganda is the only country offering a tax credit.

Expenditure-based incentives are more prone to support attracting *additional* investment than income-based incentives as they directly reduce the cost of capital of targeted investment expenses (i.e., qualifying expenditure), overall making investment projects more profitable at the margin as opposed to indiscriminately raising the profitability of already profitable projects. The tax benefit is proportional to the amount of capital invested in qualifying capital assets and current expenditures, accruing to the investor as a deduction from taxable income (i.e. tax allowance rate) or from taxes due (i.e. credit rate). In contrast, income-based incentives are typically unrelated to the amount of capital invested in qualifying expenditures and are more attractive to more profitable projects. Therefore, they do not necessarily encourage *additional* investment and may support projects that would have occurred anyways.

Expenditure-based incentives also enable targeting the reduction of costs of specific business activities that are more likely associated with positive spillovers, such as investments in capital assets (e.g. machinery and equipment), certain activities (R&D, training of employees) or job creation (Celani, Dressler and Wermelinger, 2022[4]). This targeted, cost-based approach commonly implies less revenues forgone compared to income-based tax incentives. Governments need to be careful, nonetheless, when using expenditure-based incentives; targeting decisions may correct market failures and potentially contribute to positive spillovers (e.g. increasing innovative investments through R&D incentives) but could also create distortionary effects and may require more administrative resources in their implementation than income-based alternatives (OECD, 2022[1]; Celani, Dressler and Wermelinger, 2022[4]; UN/CIAT, 2018[7]).

4.2.2. Design features suggest focus on sectors, investment size and export promotion

Eligibility conditions are widely used in EAC countries

Incentives can be designed to promote broader policy objectives, beyond investment attraction. While assessing their costs against their benefits remains crucial, well-designed incentives can help to promote sustainable economic development when adequately addressing market failures that prevent optimal outcomes (OECD, 2022[15]; Celani, Dressler and Wermelinger, 2022[4]). This can be the case, for instance, when directed at relatively underinvested locations or sectors and activities having broader positive spillovers to society (e.g., renewable energy); through eligibility conditions requiring investors or projects to fulfil certain criteria that can directly contribute to achieving specific socioeconomic goals (e.g., minimum investment amounts, minimum number of newly created jobs); or by designing incentives that curtail taxes on specific income (e.g., reduced CIT rates for export earnings) or reduce the costs of certain business activities benefiting society at large, not only the eligible investing firm (e.g., tax credits for training expenditure). Analysing these design elements provides insights into the types of investors, sectors, and activities targeted by a country and reveals which broader policy objectives are promoted by tax incentives.

EAC tax incentive design focuses on sector conditions, investment size, SEZ and outcome conditions (Figure 4.3). Similar to practices of other regions, sector conditions are the most commonly used design feature, reflected in incentives of all EAC countries (Figure 4.3, Panel A). Minimum investment requirements are used by six out of seven countries, which is proportionally higher than in all peer regions. Investment size criteria are primarily used for CIT exemptions, but as well for reduced CIT rates and tax allowances, and range from 2 million Kenyan shillings (approximately USD 14 000) for tax allowance for capital assets in Kenya to USD 50 million for a seven-year full CIT exemption in Rwanda. Governments sometimes use high investment thresholds to attract large MNEs, aiming to improve their country's reputation as a business destination, to stimulate the local economy, technology and skills transfer, and other positive FDI spillovers effects. However, minimum investment size thresholds may also discourage investment by foreign and domestic SMEs with high innovation potential (OECD, 2022[15]; OECD, 2015[16]). Some countries therefore use a staggered approach to investment size criteria and lower the threshold for SMEs, for instance, depending on a company's annual turnover (OECD, 2023[17]). A more effective approach could be to opt for expenditure-based incentives instead, as they are easier to monitor and can be designed to benefit investors proportionally to their business expenses.

Figure 4.3. Sector conditions are widely used

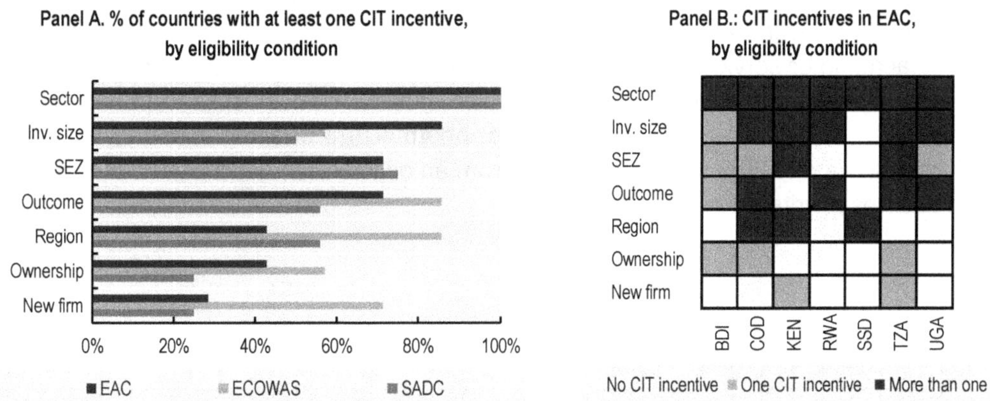

Source: OECD ITID, February 2024, based on 65 economies and 707 CIT incentive entries.

Investment location is another frequently applied eligibility criterion for incentives in the EAC, used by all Partner States except Rwanda. The DRC, Kenya and South Sudan offer incentives for investors locating in specific geographic regions, while five countries (except Rwanda and South Sudan) provide benefits for investors operating in SEZs (Figure 4.3, Panel B). Location-based incentives can target investment in SEZ or selected regions and generally give greater benefits to investments outside of capital cities, often in less developed areas. For instance, South Sudan provides an accelerated allowance for costs related to plant and machinery that increases from 50% to 75% if the project is located in least developed areas. According to an assessment of EATRs in a sample of sub-Saharan African countries, incentives in SEZs typically offer the most generous tax treatment (Celani, Dressler and Hanappi, 2022[12]).

Outcome conditions are another design mechanism to promote broader policy objectives. They are used more commonly by the EAC (in 71% of countries) than in SADC (56%) but less often than in ECOWAS (86%) (Figure 4.3, Panel A). They are linked to outcomes of the investment project, rather than characteristics of the investor or investment project. In the EAC, outcome conditions require beneficiaries to achieve certain performance results relating to a range of areas, including job creation for citizens, generating a minimum share of additional value or a minimum share of export sales. While outcome conditions can promote positive spillovers of investment and other economic goals, they require careful monitoring and administrative resources to ensure that the outcome has been achieved.

More than half (55%) of incentives offered by EAC countries require investors to meet more than one eligibility condition to benefit, while 45% of incentives require investors to meet one requirement. When multiple eligibility conditions are used, sector conditions are often combined with minimum investment or outcome conditions. When using multiple eligibility criteria, providing clear information to investors on eligibility requirements is pertinent for avoiding potential confusion and fostering transparency (see below).

Despite sector conditions, almost any sector can benefit from income-based incentives

Tax incentives can target sectors either through positive lists (determining eligible sectors), negative lists (determining which sectors are not eligible for the benefit) or a combination of both (e.g., tax incentives for manufacturing of transport vehicles, except ships and boats). Targeting through eligibility criteria deserves attention as it risks increasing distortions and administrative costs and eroding the principles of equality (IMF et al., 2015[11]).

All EAC countries use sector conditions in their tax incentive design, but almost any sector can benefit. Most sector conditions are linked to generous income-based incentives, enabling investors of almost any sector to benefit for up to ten years from significant tax breaks. Except in South Sudan, investors operating in any manufacturing sub-sector can benefit from at least one CIT exemption or reduced rate (Figure 4.4). The ITID reveals that broad manufacturing targeting is also observed in ECOWAS and SADC. Sector targeting is even broader in Kenya, Rwanda and Tanzania, where investors operating in any agricultural, mining, manufacturing or service sub-sector can benefit from incentives. Some countries operate several tax incentives with overlapping sector targeting, which can allow businesses to benefit from multiple tax incentive schemes at the same time. For example, pharmaceutical companies in Tanzania can benefit from a reduced CIT rate of 20% for five years and from an accelerated depreciation of fixed manufacturing assets that enables a write-off in two years.

Figure 4.4. Income-based incentives are available for most sectors

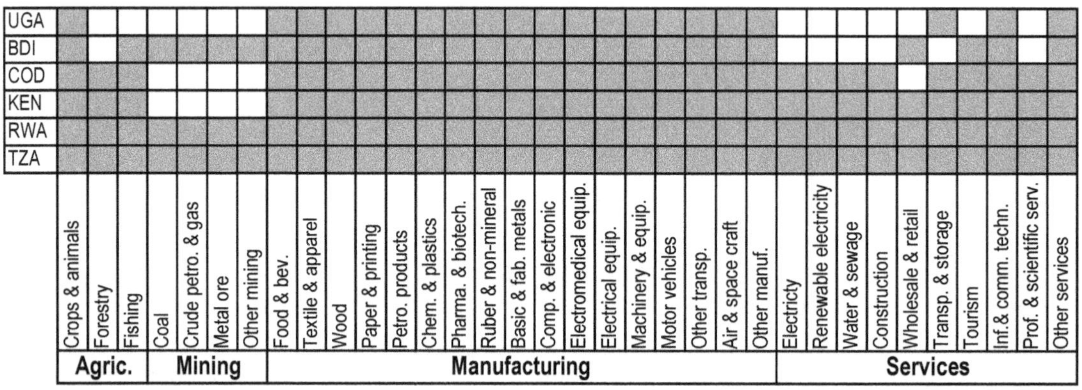

Note: Each coloured box indicates that a sub-sector can benefit from at least one income-based CIT incentive by country. The graph only reflects income-based incentives as targeting is primarily used for exemptions, but also reduced rates, and because these incentives typically involve more revenues forgone. South Sudan is not reflected as it does not offer income-based incentives. The sector classification used corresponds to the International Standard Industrial Classification of All Economic Activities (ISIC) rev. 4.
Source: Author's calculations based on OECD ITID, February 2024, based on 65 economies and 707 CIT incentive entries.

Four EAC countries (Burundi, Kenya, Rwanda, Tanzania) offer CIT incentives for extractive industries, including petroleum, metal ore and other mining. Burundi, Rwanda and Tanzania offer at least on income-based incentive available for mining operators; for instance, Rwanda offers a 15% reduced rate for registered investors in priority sectors, including processing and value addition in mining and mining activities relating to mineral exploration. Mining firms can also benefit from income-based incentives that are open to all sectors, e.g., in Tanzania, where first-time investors listed on the Dar-es-salaam Stock Exchange can benefit from a reduced rate of 25% for three years. Burundi, Kenya and Tanzania also offer accelerated depreciation or one-off deductions for exploration expenditure. While incentives during exploration periods and other taxes including royalty rates are often important for investors in extractive industries, income-based CIT incentives for mining generally appear to be both ineffective at attracting additional investment, and inefficient (i.e., costs are greater than benefits). As extractive industries are location-specific, incentives are less likely to sway investment location decisions (IGF-OECD, 2018[18]; James, 2014[10]). CIT exemptions may thus benefit firms that could have invested without incentives.

Most tax allowances also use sector conditions, targeted to enterprises operating in manufacturing, mining or tourism. They relate to capital assets like machinery and equipment used for manufacturing and mining, hotels or industrial buildings for manufacturing.

Incentives promote exports and other development objectives

Some design features and eligibility conditions of tax incentives can offer insights into the intended objectives of policy measures. The ITID identifies certain economic and social development goals that are supported through design features of tax incentives, such as job creation, social inclusion, job quality and skills development, promoting exports and improving the environmental impact of businesses (Figure 4.5). Such goals can be promoted through outcome conditions (e.g., creating a minimum number of jobs) or targeting certain sectors (e.g., renewable energy sector). CIT incentives can also encourage these goals by supporting certain activities via qualifying expenditure (e.g., tax allowances for training expenditure) or qualifying income (e.g., reduced CIT rate for export income). As per the ITID methodology, CIT incentive schemes having no related outcome or eligibility condition, or qualifying expenditure/income explicitly linked to any of such development goals are not considered to explicitly support such goals, even though their existence and underlying motivation might relate to such development objectives.

Figure 4.5. CIT incentive design features target exports among other development goals

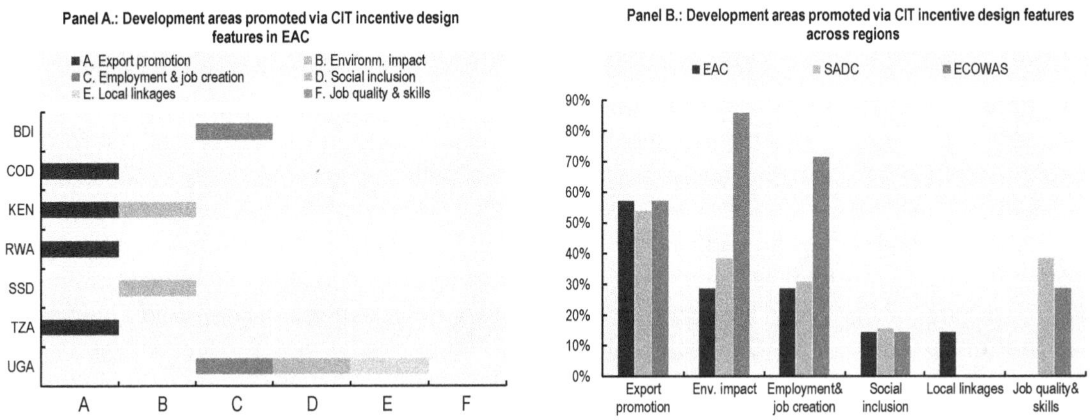

Note: The ITID identifies development goals that are commonly targeted through CIT incentive design features which include the six areas shown in the figure. For more information on the indicator methodology, please refer to Annex B.
Source: OECD ITID, February 2024, based on 65 economies and 707 CIT incentive entries.

All EAC countries have at least one CIT incentive in place with design features supporting broader policy objectives (Figure 4.5, Panel A). The three areas supported in most countries are export promotion (in four out of seven countries, mostly by requiring a minimum share of export revenues), employment and job creation (in two out of seven countries, by requiring a minimum number of new jobs created and hiring a minimum share of people with disabilities), and improving the environmental impact of investment (in two out of seven countries, by targeting water/waste management and recycling). For instance, Burundi lowers the preferential rate for free zone companies to 10% instead of 15%, if investors create at least 100 jobs for citizens. In the DRC, manufacturing companies with at least 20% of export turnover are eligible for accelerated depreciation, enabling depreciation of 60% of a fixed asset's value in first year of use. Kenya, Rwanda and Tanzania also use minimum export turnover thresholds but offer ten-year tax exemptions for Export Processing Zone companies (in Kenya and Tanzania) and a reduced CIT rate of 25% (in Rwanda). Kenya and South Sudan offer initial allowances for capital assets for companies operating in selected sectors, including water and waste management (Kenya and South Sudan), and reduction of environmental damage (Kenya).

One incentive can be designed to support multiple policy goals. For instance, Uganda offers a tax credit that enables investors to deduct 2% income tax due, if at least 5% of their workers have disabilities, thereby supporting both employment and social inclusion. Uganda also offers a CIT exemption for investors that use at least 70% of locally sourced raw materials and employ at least 70% EAC citizens who must take up at least 70% of the wage bill, thereby encouraging local linkages and employment.

The areas most supported in EAC are also the same development areas in ECOWAS and SADC, although in peer regions a higher share of countries have designed incentives in a way that explicitly targets employment and job creation and improving the environmental impact of businesses (Figure 4.5, Panel B).

In contrast to peer regions, EAC countries do not offer CIT incentives that support job creation and skills development through design features. Some countries in peer regions design incentives to promote employer-sponsored training of their workforce, e.g., through a tax allowance that enhances the deductible amount of a firm's training expenditures for employees. Well-designed incentives targeting skills development can provide an additional support to raising workforce qualification and labour productivity (IMF et al., 2015[11]). For example, investors in Botswana can deduct 200% of training cost spent for their employees for training programmes approved by the Commissioner.

Looking forward, EAC governments could consider revising some of their incentives to maximise positive spillovers, limit potentially excessive benefits to investors, and ensure incentives are in line with broader investment policy goals. Incentives policies should carefully weigh benefits against costs and monitor if benefits actually materialise. Governments should also investigate if other measures, including investment promotion and facilitation activities and other regulatory activities, could be more appropriate than CIT incentives to support certain economic and sustainable development objectives (OECD, 2022[15]). Joining global initiatives, such as Tax Inspectors Without Borders or the OECD/G20 Inclusive Framework on BEPS could support EAC countries in enhancing their tax systems and capacity. To foster regional co-operation and support countries' transition to smarter and more cost-effective incentive policies, EAC Partner States could consider establishing a forum for exchanging on their incentives strategies and design approaches, as well as on broader tax policy and administration matters. For example, the regional platform for tax co-operation for Latin America and the Caribbean (PTLAC) was recently established to enable cross-national dialogue on challenging tax policy matters between Ministers of Treasury, Economy and Finance. During the first year of operation, PTLAC's Technical Working Group established sub-working groups on tax benefits, environmental taxation and progressivity (CEPAL, 2024[19]). The OECD and other partners could provide support for such dialogues. Peer-learning and dialogue may help to prevent a race-to-the-bottom in tax competition through investment incentives.

4.3. Enhancing transparency of incentive frameworks

Transparency of incentives involves the governance of incentives, including how incentives are authorised and awarded, whether eligibility criteria are clearly stated in laws and the level of discretion authorities have in selecting which investors receive incentives. It is also an important element for fostering accountability about public expenditure and for policy evaluations (OECD, 2023[20]). Transparency further involves investment facilitation and how clearly and available incentive-relevant information is communicated, which is one of the challenges identified in the EAC Investment Policy; although Partner States' IPAs provide services and information on incentives, these resources are not well known by investors. They end up having to rely on professional services companies to navigate information which could have been provided directly by the IPAs.

Enhancing the transparency of their incentive regimes is challenging for many governments but EAC Partner States have already taken steps to do so. Most countries provide English translations of their incentive-granting legislation. While Burundi and the DRC provide French laws, Rwanda's Investment Promotion and Facilitation Law 2021 is available in English, French and Kinyarwanda. Foreign investors unfamiliar with the local market may not be fully aware of the support available, particularly if incentives are granted by different authorities or different legal sources (e.g., in Burundi), or if laws are not harmonised (e.g., in South Sudan).[2] An important transparency-enhancing tax reform for many EAC countries would be to publish consolidated laws, in which all amendments have been incorporated and to consolidate all tax-related legislative provisions into a single act (e.g. the Income Tax Ordinance), reflecting available tax incentives granted through other laws.

The EAC Investment Policy outlines information on incentives in Partner States and some governments already published incentive-relevant information or tax incentive guides (e.g., the Uganda Revenue

Authority) (EAC, 2019[3]; Uganda Revenues Authority, 2023[21]). The EAC homepage also operates a dedicated section on investment incentives but does not reflect the latest policy changes and could further elaborate on the necessary requirements that investors have to meet (Uganda Revenues Authority, 2023[21]; EAC, n.d.[22]). These efforts go into the right direction but could be enhanced by implementing an EAC incentives guide, client charter or platform that highlights up-to-date information and the full scope of benefits, including eligibility criteria, granting procedures and practical guidance (e.g., scope of eligible costs, whether incentive apply when businesses start operating or become profitable, etc). The EAC Investment Policy could be enriched by referring to such a platform, which can provide more details on individual benefits and is easier to update on amendments than a five-year strategic document, facilitating navigating through the EAC incentive frameworks for investors.

4.4. Monitoring and evaluation are crucial to understand incentive effectiveness

Monitoring and evaluations are crucial for understanding whether incentives effectively achieve their policy objectives and at what cost. The EAC Investment Policy lists developing a mechanism for monitoring and evaluation as one of its objectives, but it is unclear to which extent it has advanced. Monitoring includes tracking data on the use of incentives, beneficiaries, outcomes, and costs. Monitoring should also include scrutinising investor compliance with eligibility criteria, for example, through collecting evidence that shows respective requirements (e.g., job creation) were met or by conducting audits to uncover potential fraud or abuse. The collected information can assist in determining if the incentive is contributing to development goals and provide a data foundation for evaluations. Some EAC countries already anchored monitoring responsibilities in the law, for instance, Article 30 of Burundi's investment law states that the investment agency should maintain a database on all investors established in the country and monitor investment projects to ensure that incentives are targeted at projects that meet the required conditions (Republique du Burundi, 2021[23]).

A first step towards evaluations involves mapping all existing incentives, their policy objectives, and legal references. The EAC Investment Policy already provides high-level information on incentives in Partner States and could be used to start this exercise (EAC, 2019[3]). By clearly stating policy goals, governments can regularly scrutinise if the stated objectives of tax incentives, such as directing investment into specific sectors or activities, align with investment promotion strategies and national development targets. This mapping should also include information on incentive uptake and characteristics of beneficiary firms, which can provide important insights into how incentives are used and if incentives appear to be supporting projects most in need. Most EAC countries require investors to file application for incentives, which could be used to obtain such data. Such an exercise could bring more clarity on benefitting economic actors and could be useful for identifying any potential redundancies, incongruencies and inefficiencies.

Regular reporting of tax expenditures helps governments to compare how these benefits of incentives measure against costs and creates accountability and better control over the use of public funds (OECD et al., 2023[24]). Positively, the Global Tax Expenditure Database shows that all EAC countries (except South Sudan) engage in tax expenditure reporting. CIT expenditures in EAC significantly reduce public revenues, amounting to 0.5% of GDP in Rwanda, 0.14% in Uganda and 0.18% in Kenya in 2021. Burundi reported different types of taxes but not income taxes, while Tanzania only reported tax expenditure related to taxes on goods and services. The DRC's last reporting year was 2020, indicating CIT expenditure amounting to 0.02% of GDP (Redonda, von Haldenwang and Aliu, 2023[25]). Such reporting reflects important developments for fostering public transparency on costs of incentive programmes and as a key step towards cost-benefit analysis. Tax expenditure reporting could further be enhanced by reporting on costs of specific incentives (provision-level data), which would provide essential data for assessing the performance of individual incentives (Redonda, Von Haldenwang and Aliu, 2021[26]).

In the longer-term, EAC governments could consider undertaking a full-fledged assessment of the impact of the incentives schemes to understand if they have contributed to achieving their intended objectives, for instance in terms of exports, jobs, wages, skills and other outcomes in different regions. A joint evaluation mechanism, as outlined as an objective in the EAC Investment Policy, could foster government co-operation on identifying redundant incentives and rationalising them, in a view to strengthening national revenues that can be critical for tackling more structural investment climate weaknesses.

References

Abramovsky, L. et al. (2018), "Are corporate tax incentives for investment fit for purpose? Revisiting economic principles and evidence from low- and middle-income countries", https://doi.org/10.1920/RE.IFS.2018.0142. [14]

ATAF (2023), , *ATAF & the South Sudan National Revenue Authority Launch Technical Assistance Programme*, https://www.ataftax.org/ataf-the-south-sudan-national-revenue-authority-launch-technical-assistance-programme. [8]

Celani, A., L. Dressler and T. Hanappi (2022), "Assessing tax relief from targeted investment tax incentives through corporate effective tax rates: Methodology and initial findings for seven Sub-Saharan African countries", *OECD Taxation Working Papers*, No. 58, OECD Publishing, Paris, https://doi.org/10.1787/22235558. [12]

Celani, A., L. Dressler and M. Wermelinger (2022), "Building an Investment Tax Incentives database: Methodology and initial findings for 36 developing countries", *OECD Working Papers on International Investment*, No. 2022/01, OECD Publishing, Paris, https://doi.org/10.1787/62e075a9-en. [4]

CEPAL (2024), *Countries that Make Up the Regional Platform for Tax Cooperation in Latin America and the Caribbean Issue Joint Statement in Support of Brazil's G20 Presidency*, http://www.cepal.org/en/pressreleases/countries-make-regional-platform-tax-cooperation-latin-america-and-caribbean-issue. [19]

EAC (2019), *East African Community Investment Policy*. [3]

EAC (2000), *Treaty for the Establishment of the EAC*, https://investmentpolicy.unctad.org/international-investment-agreements/treaty-files/2487/download. [2]

EAC (n.d.), *Investment Incentives*, https://www.eac.int/investment-climate-and-incentives/investment-incentives. [22]

IGF-OECD (2018), *Tax Incentives in Mining: Minimising risks to revenue*, Intergovernmental Forum on Mining, Minerals, Metals and Sustainable Development (IGF) and OECD, https://www.oecd.org/tax/beps/tax-incentives-in-mining-minimising-risks-to-revenue-oecd-igf.pdf (accessed on 8 March 2023). [18]

IMF/OECD (2017), *Tax Certainty: IMF/OECD Report for the G20 Finance Ministers*, IMF/OECD, https://www.oecd.org/tax/tax-policy/tax-certainty-report-oecd-imf-report-g20-finance-ministers-march-2017.pdf. [6]

IMF et al. (2015), *Options for Low Income Countries' Effective and Efficient Use of Ta Incentives for Investment, A report to the G-20 Development Working Group*. [11]

James, S. (2014), *Tax and Non-Tax Incentives and Investments: Evidence and Policy Implications*, World Bank, Washington DC, https://papers.ssrn.com/sol3/papers.cfm?abstract_id=2401905. [10]

Klemm, A. and S. Van Parys (2012), "Empirical evidence on the effects of tax incentives", *International Tax and Public Finance*, Vol. 12, pp. 393–423, https://doi.org/10.1007/s10797-011-9194-8. [13]

OECD (2023), *FDI Qualities Review of Croatia: Advancing the Strategic Framework for Investment Promotion and Facilitation*, OECD Publishing, Paris, https://doi.org/10.1787/79b2345b-en. [17]

OECD (2023), *Global Revenue Statistics Database*, OECD Publishing, Paris, https://stats.oecd.org/Index.aspx?DataSetCode=RS_GBL (accessed on 13 September 2024). [9]

OECD (2023), "Improving transparency of incentives for investment facilitation", *OECD Business and Finance Policy Papers*, No. 35, OECD Publishing, Paris, https://doi.org/10.1787/ab40a2f1-en. [20]

OECD (2022), *FDI Qualities Policy Toolkit*, OECD Publishing, Paris, https://doi.org/10.1787/7ba74100-en. [15]

OECD (2022), *Tax Incentives and the Global Minimum Corporate Tax: Reconsidering Tax Incentives after the GloBE Rules*, OECD Publishing, Paris, https://doi.org/10.1787/25d30b96-en. [1]

OECD (2015), *Policy Guidance for Investment in Clean Energy Infrastructure: Expanding Access to Clean Energy for Green Growth and Development*, OECD Publishing, Paris, https://doi.org/10.1787/9789264212664-en. [16]

OECD et al. (2023), *Revenue Statistics in Latin America and the Caribbean 2023*, OECD Publishing, Paris, https://doi.org/10.1787/a7640683-en. [24]

Redonda, A., C. Von Haldenwang and F. Aliu (2021), "Tax Expenditure Reporting and Domestic Revenue Mobilization in Africa", in Mosquera Valderrama, I., D. Lesage and W. Lips (eds.), *Taxation, International Cooperation and the 2030 Sustainable Development Agenda*, Springer, https://doi.org/10.1007/978-3-030-64857-2_9. [26]

Redonda, A., C. von Haldenwang and F. Aliu (2023), *Global Tax Expenditures Database [data set], Version 1.2.1.*, https://doi.org/10.5281/zenodo.8337951. [25]

Republique du Burundi (2021), *Loi Nr.1/19 du 27 juin 2021 portant modification de la loi Nr.1/24 du 10 Septembre 2008 portant Code des Investissements du Burundi*, https://www.droit-afrique.com/uploads/Burundi-Code-2021-investissements.pdf. [23]

Uganda Revenues Authority (2023), *Tax Incentives Guide*, https://ura.go.ug/download-category/investors-guides/# (accessed on 13 September 2024). [21]

UN/CIAT (2018), *Design and Assessment of Tax Incentives in Developing Countries: Selected Issues and a Country Experience*, United Nations, https://www.un.org/esa/ffd/wp-content/uploads/2018/02/tax-incentives_eng.pdf. [7]

UNIDO (2013), *Africa Investor Survey*, United Nations Industrial Development Organization. [5]

Notes

[1] Tax incentives data registered in the OECD ITID and subject to this analysis for ECOWAS includes: Côte d'Ivoire, Gambia, Ghana, Liberia, Nigeria, Senegal, Sierra Leone; for SADC: Angola, Botswana, Comoros, the DRC, Eswatini, Lesotho, Madagascar, Malawi, Mauritius, Mozambique, Namibia, Seychelles, South Africa, Tanzania, Zambia and Zimbabwe.

[2] South Sudan's Taxation Act 2009 and its Investment Promotion Act 2009 are not harmonised which provides challenges in understanding whether incentives are still in place. Tax incentives (capital allowances) are granted in the Investment Promotion Act 2009, while the Taxation Act 2009 and some of its amendments (e.g., Taxation Amendment Act, 2016) mention that exemptions and alternative methods from business profit tax, including but not limited to, provisions of the Investment Promotion Act, that are not granted via the Taxation Act, are void.

5 Promoting and enabling responsible business conduct

This chapter highlights the importance of responsible business conduct (RBC) for the EAC region and presents the key elements of RBC. It then provides an overview and analysis of policies and initiatives relevant to RBC at both regional and national levels within the EAC.

Promoting and enabling responsible business conduct (RBC) is key to attract quality investment and ensure that business activity contributes to sustainable development. In recent years, the growing attention paid to RBC by governments worldwide through both legislation and policy measures, and the increasing importance of environmental, social and governance concerns for investor and consumer decision-making, have turned RBC into an increasingly important factor to remain internationally competitive as an investment and a sourcing destination. In the EAC, the aim of attracting responsible investment and achieving sustainable development is laid out throughout main strategic policies. But key economic sectors of the region still face RBC risks related to human and labour rights, environmental protection, and integrity. While civil society and businesses have started to address RBC issues, there exists a disparity in the pace at which governments and stakeholders are advancing on this agenda. Further government action is needed to implement and enforce relevant legislation and policies, develop policy frameworks relevant for RBC, and enhance businesses' awareness and capacity to conduct risk-based due diligence.

5.1. Relevance of RBC to promote responsible and sustainable investment

Promoting and enabling responsible business practices in the EAC is important in light of the structure of the economies of Partner States' and their trade and investment linkages, which depend strongly on the minerals and agriculture sectors. As these sectors are prone to risks of adverse impacts related to human and labour rights, the environment, or integrity, international standards and practical guidance on RBC can help governments and businesses prevent and address these risks. This section lays out the relevance of RBC for the EAC region, before providing information on the key elements and concepts of RBC.

5.1.1. RBC is relevant for key economic sectors in the EAC

RBC establishes the expectation that all businesses, regardless of their legal status, size, ownership structure, or sector, should address and avoid the adverse impacts of their operations on people, the planet, and society, while contributing to sustainable development wherever they operate. This entails that businesses must assess the risks related to human and labour rights, the environment, and integrity arising from or associated with their activities, supply chains, and business relationships.

RBC is particularly relevant for the seven examined EAC Partner States due to the structure of their economies, heavily reliant on natural resources and agricultural products whose exploitation and production may give rise to RBC risks. The EAC is home to important reserves of mineral resources such as cobalt, coltan and gold, the DRC, Tanzania, and Rwanda being among the main mineral-producing countries in the world (EAC, n.d.[1]; EAC, n.d.[2]). The Great Lakes Region, which comprises most EAC countries, produces nearly half the world's coltan and is home to some of the largest cobalt, copper and lithium deposits (ILO, 2019[3]; OECD, 2019[4]). The DRC is the largest cobalt producer, with 70% of the world's resources. Overall, the minerals and extractive industries hold significant importance for the economy, employment, and foreign currency earnings of the region (EAC, n.d.[5]). Agriculture is also an important sector for the EAC's economy and development. According to the EAC Development Strategy 2021/22-2025/26, in the majority of EAC economies, agriculture is the most important source of employment, providing over 70% of employment opportunities, contributing to 65% of the volume of intra-regional trade and more than 25% to the GDP of EAC countries (EAC, 2021[6]).

RBC is also key for the EAC in light of its Partner States' integration into global value chains and the prevalence of natural resources and agricultural products in their exports. According to the latest EAC Trade and Investment Report (2022), "the region is highly dependent on export of primary agricultural and mineral commodities with little value addition" (EAC, 2022[7]). Primary mineral and agricultural products are the most traded and exported products in the EAC. Mineral products accounted for 28% of the Community's total trade in 2023.[1]

As in other regions, the minerals and agriculture sectors in the EAC have historically been linked to various RBC issues. Agriculture is linked both globally and in the EAC to the most child labour and deforestation, with major concerns, for example, in tea and coffee production in Kenya, Rwanda, Tanzania and Uganda. Estimates of overall child labour rates in EAC countries are as high as 31% in Burundi and 25% in Tanzania according to ILO and UNICEF (UNICEF, 2023[8]).[2] In the minerals and extractive sector, human and labour rights abuses including child labour and unsafe working conditions, as well as corruption and armed conflict are major concerns in the region. Workers in these sectors often face unsafe working conditions and economic exploitation, as reported in gold supply chains in Tanzania or cobalt and coltan supply chains in the DRC (ILO, 2019[3]). Although there is no sufficient data on the prevalence of child labour in the mining sector in the EAC, surveys have found children present at 30% of visited artisanal and small-scale mining (ASM) sites in the DRC (BGR, 2019[9]). Mining also contributes to adverse impacts on health in EAC Partner States, with the proliferation of lung diseases among workers and communities being observed in both ASM and industrial large-scale mining (NEPAD, 2023[10]).

In some countries, businesses in the extractive sector are also at risk of contributing to armed conflict, violence, and corruption, as it has been reported extensively for the Great Lakes Region in relation to tin, tantalum, tungsten and gold production. Similar examples relate to gold and oil extraction in South Sudan and copper and cobalt supply chains in the DRC (UNSC, 2023[11]; UNSC, 2020[12]; GI-TOC, 2023[13]). Since 2021, there has been a resurgence of armed group activity in Eastern DRC involved in mineral smuggling and human rights abuses connected to the extractive sector, with such groups alleged in some cases to have links to and receive support from governments of the region (UNSC, 2023[14]).

While countries in the region have made commitments, for example, to fostering peace and stability through improving governance of the minerals sector a reported lack of implementation causes harm to the conditions for investment in the region. Promoting and enabling responsible business practices in the EAC region is therefore key to prevent and address these issues. This, in turn, can support the EAC Development Strategy and Investment Policy to increase FDI and trade levels, as investment and trade partners in the region and worldwide increasingly pay attention to sustainability matters and have taken measures to promote sustainable and responsible supply chains, either through legislation or policy measures (EAC, 2021[6]). According to an OECD survey on FDI decisions, adequate legislation in the areas of human rights, labour rights, environment and anti-corruption is one of the key factors to stimulate investment in the agri-food sector (Punthakey, 2020[15]). Regional data analyses have further found that African and EAC economies having companies with robust responsible business practices, including on anti-corruption, tend to attract more FDI (Agyemang, et al, 2020[16]). Likewise, analysis suggests that conducting risk-based due diligence to address adverse impacts on human rights and the environment can benefit not only companies, but also supply chain resilience, and more broadly contribute to achieving sustainability goals. For example, the UN Group of Experts on the DRC has found that due diligence programmes have improved transparency in the tin, tungsten and tantalum sector in the Great Lakes Region in East Africa (UNSC, 2020[12]). Other studies highlight that, in areas where such programmes exist, military interference in mining has decreased and public revenues have increased (IPS, 2020[17]).

5.1.2. Key elements of RBC

The three main international instruments on RBC

The three main international instruments that have become key references for responsible business practices globally are the OECD Guidelines for Multinational Enterprises on Responsible Business Conduct (the OECD MNE Guidelines), the UN Guiding Principles on Business and Human Rights (UNGPs), and the ILO Tripartite Declaration of Principles concerning Multinational Enterprises and Social Policy. These instruments are aligned with and complement each other (UN et al., 2019[18]).

The OECD MNE Guidelines is the most comprehensive government-backed instrument guiding business action on sustainable development and addressing adverse impacts associated with their operations and supply chains on people, the planet, and society. They have undergone continuous updates since their introduction in 1976 to ensure their relevance considering changing societal challenges and the evolving international business landscape. The latest update in 2023 aligns the OECD MNE Guidelines with internationally agreed goals on climate change and biodiversity as well as latest developments in technology and due diligence recommendations to all forms of corruption.

The OECD MNE Guidelines are part of the OECD Declaration on International Investment and Multinational Enterprises, which has 51 adherent countries, with Mauritius soon to become the 52nd. These countries have set up a unique implementation mechanism: the National Contact Points for Responsible Business Conduct (NCP), which promote the OECD MNE Guidelines and act as non-judicial grievance mechanisms for alleged violations of the Guidelines in cases referred to as "specific instances". While EAC countries have not formally adhered to the OECD MNE Guidelines, between 2002 and 2023, 51 specific instances have been submitted to NCPs of adherent countries concerning business operations in EAC Partner States. Most of these cases concern the mining sector in the DRC and are linked to human rights, labour and environmental issues.

Risk-based due diligence

Due diligence is a critical component of RBC. It implies that companies identify, prevent, and mitigate adverse impacts and be accountable for addressing them. This process involves not only preventing and mitigating potential adverse impacts caused by a company's own operations, but also addressing risks that may arise along its supply chain, thus giving all companies along the supply chain a role in the due diligence process.

The OECD Due Diligence Guidance for Responsible Business Conduct recommends a six-step process for conducting risk-based due diligence that can be applied by any enterprise, regardless of its size, location, or industry. The steps outlined in the guidance include integrating RBC into the enterprise's policies and management systems, identifying and assessing adverse impacts, taking actions to cease, prevent, or mitigate adverse impacts, monitoring the implementation and results of these actions, communicating how impacts are addressed, and providing or cooperating in remediation when necessary.

In addition to the overarching OECD Due Diligence Guidance for Responsible Business Conduct, the OECD has developed specific recommendations for various high-risk sectors, including agriculture, minerals, garment and footwear, and finance (OECD, 2018[19]). These sector-specific Guidances aim to help enterprises implement due diligence effectively in these different sectors through concrete advice and examples. Recently, the OECD also released handbooks to support companies in their efforts to embed considerations on specific RBC risks, such as deforestation, child labour and forced labour, into their due diligence processes (OECD, 2023[20]; OECD, 2023[21]; OECD/FAO, 2023[22]).

Role of Government in Promoting RBC

In recent years, there has been a growing recognition that governments play a key role in supporting the effective implementation of RBC principles and standards by providing an enabling legal and policy environment, creating incentives, and exemplifying RBC in their own activities. To reflect this, in 2023, the OECD released the Recommendation on the Role of Government in Promoting Responsible Business Conduct (the OECD Recommendation on the Role of Government), to which 51 countries and the European Union have adhered to. It lays out a set of 21 principles and policy recommendations to assist governments, other public authorities, and relevant stakeholders in their efforts to design and implement policies that enable and promote RBC (OECD, 2023[23]).

The role that governments play in promoting RBC is evidenced by the increasing number of laws and policy initiatives related to sustainability and RBC. This includes both mandatory frameworks (e.g. legislation on non-financial disclosure, trade-based measures and conducting due diligence), as well as voluntary measures (e.g. government guidance and other government-led initiatives) (OECD, 2024[24]). To date, 75% of OECD countries have either adopted or are in the process of adopting legislation containing due diligence requirements. This legislation often makes reference to international RBC principles and standards. For example, in the minerals sector, the OECD Due Diligence Guidance for Responsible Supply Chains of Minerals from Conflict-Affected and High-Risk Areas (the OECD Minerals Guidance) has been referred to in various legal frameworks, notably in the United States and the European Union, as well as in some EAC Partner States, such as the DRC and Rwanda. In the United States, Section 1502 of the Dodd-Frank Act requires that due diligence be conducted in relation to tin, tantalum, tungsten and gold originating from six EAC Partner States (Burundi, the DRC, Rwanda, South Sudan, Tanzania, and Uganda). In the European Union, the Conflict Minerals Regulation (EU) 2017/821 introduced due diligence requirements for tin, tantalum, tungsten and gold sourced from any country or area that is conflict-affected or high-risk. These requirements have been further complemented by the 2023 Batteries Regulation, which requires the conduct of due diligence for critical raw materials used in batteries (IEA, 2023[25]).

5.2. Promoting and enabling RBC in the EAC

Some businesses and other stakeholders in the EAC are increasingly aware of the importance of RBC and have started to develop relevant initiatives to promote responsible business practices. The EAC has put in place regional policy frameworks, both thematic and sectorial, that provide relevant entry points for RBC. However, in general, governments do not explicitly define the role of the private sector vis-a-vis human and labour rights, environmental or integrity issues. The EAC and its Partner States can thus play a more active role in creating an enabling environment for RBC. This section first explores awareness of RBC among businesses and stakeholders in the region before analysing the existing legal and policy frameworks to promote and enable RBC, both at the EAC regional and national level.

5.2.1. Business and other stakeholders in the EAC have started promoting RBC

Businesses and other stakeholders (including civil society, workers' organisations and multi-stakeholder initiatives) in the EAC are increasingly aware of the importance of adopting responsible business practices (see overview in Annex C). Large companies and business organisations tend to be familiar with RBC and have started developing related initiatives. UN Global Compact regional networks exist in the DRC, Kenya, Rwanda and Tanzania. A total of 365 companies participate in these networks, which work to promote sustainable development as well as business action in the areas of human and labour rights, protection of the environment, and anti-corruption. In Kenya, for instance, the network is led by the Kenya Association of Manufacturers, the Kenya Private Sector Alliance, and the Federation of Kenya Employers, and it carries out various initiatives such as providing tools, advice and training relating to the SDGs, climate action, and gender equality (UNGC, 2021[26]). Moreover, in several EAC Partner States, business and industry organisations have developed RBC-related programmes and guidance. Relevant examples include the Guidance on Corporate Social Responsibility in the Mining Sector in Katanga prepared by the Mining Chamber in the DRC (Chambre des Mines), which provides information on how to implement corporate social responsibility strategies relating to specific issues such as human and labour rights, the environment, or fair operating practices (GIZ/ FEC, 2016[27]). Over the last years, MNEs operating in minerals supply chains in the EAC have also been involved in due diligence initiatives.[3] While the implementation of these initiatives has been challenging so far, businesses and other stakeholders continue to promote collaborative action to support due diligence efforts (OECD, 2015[28]).

Civil society organisations (CSOs) and trade unions in the EAC also play a role in promoting RBC. For example, the Legal and Human Rights Centre in Tanzania has set up a "Human Rights and Business" programme which seeks to promote RBC in line with international RBC instruments, including the UNGPs and the OECD MNE Guidelines (LHRC, 2022[29]). The Uganda Consortium on Corporate Responsibility is another CSO that aims to enhance private sector accountability in cases of business-related violations of economic, social and cultural rights (UCCA, n.d.[30]). Trade unions in the EAC also advocate for workers' rights and negotiate collective bargaining agreements. The trade unions of Kenya, Uganda, Zanzibar, Tanzania, Rwanda and Burundi are members of the East African Trade Union Confederation (EATUC), which has observer status within the EAC structure, and has developed a strategy to advocate for workers' rights in trade and investment frameworks (EATUC, n.d.[31]; EATUC, 2021[32]).

Awareness-raising and promotion of responsible business practices in the EAC has also made progress thanks to multi-stakeholder initiatives. Over the last years, various multi-stakeholder initiatives have started promoting RBC and the observance of the OECD Due Diligence Guidance, in particular in the mining sector. Relevant initiatives include workshops by the Rwandan National Commission for Human Rights, jointly organised with OHCHR and the Ministry of Commerce, to strengthen stakeholders' capacity to address business-related human rights violations (FES, 2022[33]). The Project Access by the Impact Facility, for instance, is a multi-stakeholder partnership of CSOs, communities and companies in the gold supply chain in East Africa (The Impact Facility, n.d.[34]).

5.2.2. The EAC has adopted some policy frameworks relevant for RBC

Beyond the promotion by businesses and other stakeholders, the adoption of responsible business practices in the EAC can be facilitated by government action both at the regional and national levels. As highlighted in the OECD Recommendation on the Role of Government, governments have a key role to play in the creation of enabling legal and policy environments for RBC. At the regional level, the EAC has developed policies, including overarching, thematic, and sector-specific ones, that are relevant to enable RBC, although there are so far no specific policies or initiatives on RBC or business and human rights.

Overarching policy frameworks at EAC level do not address RBC

The EAC has developed common policy frameworks to promote investment and trade in the region. These frameworks broadly refer to issues such as human rights, the environment, and sustainable development. The comprehensive EAC Vision 2050, for instance, aims to achieve the sustainable use of natural resources, improve environmental management and conservation, as well as promoting sustainable agricultural production, good governance, and human rights. It also refers to addressing social and environmental issues in the agriculture and mining sectors (EAC, 2016[35]). Similarly, the 6th EAC Development Strategy 2021/22-2025/26 sets out the objective to protect human rights and the environment (EAC, 2021[6]). Yet, none of these documents recognise the role of the private sector in promoting sustainable development outcomes.

Beyond these strategic documents, the EAC adopted a regional Investment Policy in 2019, which provides non-binding guidance to EAC countries on investment protection, promotion, and facilitation. The guiding principles of this policy refer to "responsible and sustainable investments" as well as to the SDGs, but the policy does not include any definitions or specific policy measures to encourage responsible business practices by investors.

The EAC also developed a Model Investment Code in 2006, which remains the reference for the design of national investment policies and laws. It provides foreign investors with national treatment non-discrimination but does not include any specific sustainability provisions or expectations regarding investors' behaviour. The only provision related to RBC is an article pursuant to which investment promotion agencies shall coordinate "the carrying out of an environment impact assessment study of the enterprise as required under the relevant environment laws" when issuing registration certificates (EAC, 2006[36]).

As discussed in Chapter 2, a Model Investment Treaty was adopted by the EAC in 2016 to provide guidance to Partner States for investment treaty negotiation. This Model includes a range of sustainability provisions, which aim to promote human rights, labour rights, the environment, and anti-corruption. Beyond references to sustainable development and human rights in the preamble, it includes provisions on the right to regulate "consistent with the goals and principles of sustainable development" (Article 15) and on the "right to pursue development goals" that deal with the environment and labour rights. On the environment, this article provides that the parties shall not incentivise investment "by relaxing or waiving domestic environmental legislation" and that "investors shall, in performing their activities, protect the environment and where the activity causes damages to the environment, [...] restore it to the extent appropriate and feasible". In relation to labour rights, it provides that host states "shall ensure that investment does not waive or derogate from labour rights" and that "investors shall comply with international conventions and existing labour policies, and, in particular, not use child labour and support for the elimination of all sort of child labour including forced or compulsory labour" (Article 16). Moreover, the Model Investment Treaty includes a provision, which states that the assessment of an investor's compensation should take into account "any harm or damage that the investor or its investment has caused to the environment or local community that have not been remedied by the investor or the investment" (Article 7). Further relevant articles refer also to an anti-corruption obligation by investors (Article 11) (EAC, 2016[37]).

The EAC established the Consultative Dialogue Framework (CDF) in 2012 to institutionalise public-private dialogue. This framework facilitates structured dialogue between the EAC, private sector organisations, civil society, and other interest groups. It aims to promote inclusive and consultative stakeholder engagement in the EAC integration process and presents a potential framework to promote RBC. The CDF provides for national dialogues through the national ministries responsible for the EAC, while regional dialogues take place through the EAC Secretariat. At the regional level, the recognised stakeholders for engagement are represented by the East African Civil Society Organisations Forum and the East Africa Business Council. As part of the CDF, an annual EAC Secretary General's Forum is held, which brings together civil society and private sector organisations across the region to develop recommendations to the Council of Ministers (EAC, n.d.[38]). The EAC has put in place thematic frameworks in key areas related to RBC.

The EAC has developed legal and policy frameworks on areas such as human rights, labour rights, the environment, anti-corruption, and consumer interests (Table 5.1). While these frameworks are part of the enabling environment for RBC, most of them could be more specific on the role of the private sector in these different areas.

Table 5.1. EAC thematic policy frameworks relevant for RBC

EAC framework	Date	Content
Human rights		
EAC Gender Policy	2018	The EAC Gender Policy aims to promote gender equality within the Community through various objectives. These include enhancing co-ordination and reporting on gender equality commitments, integrating gender concerns into all sectors of planning and budgeting, increasing women's participation in political and decision-making processes, ensuring equitable access to resources and participation in regional trade, addressing gender-based violence and harmful cultural practices, and involving women in peace and security efforts.
EAC Gender Equality and Development Bill	2016	The EAC Gender Equality and Development Bill aims to consolidate and harmonise the various commitments on gender equality that have been made at regional, continental and international levels in the context of the EAC.
Labour rights		
EAC Child Policy	2016	The EAC Child Policy aims to promote the rights of children to survival, development, protection and participation.

EAC framework	Date	Content
Environment		
EAC Regional Bioeconomy Strategy 2021/22-2031/32	2021	The EAC Regional Bioeconomy Strategy aims to promote food security and sustainable agriculture, health and well-being, biobased industrial development, and sustainable energy.
EAC Forests Management and Protection Bill	2015	The EAC Forests Management and Protection Bill provides for the management and protection of national forests and trans-boundary forest ecosystems in the EAC.
EAC Climate Change Policy	2011	The Climate Change Policy aims to address the adverse impacts of climate change in the region by widening and deepening co-operation among Partner States.
EAC Transboundary Ecosystems Management Bill	2010	The EAC Transboundary Ecosystems Management Bill provides a legal framework to enhance the quality of the environment and ensure sustainable use of shared natural resources in the EAC.
EAC Protocol on Environment and Natural Resources Management	2006 (currently being revised)	The EAC Protocol on Environment and Natural Resources Management aims to promote the sustainable use and management of the environment and natural resources.
Anti-corruption		
The East African Integrity and Anticorruption Bill	2019	The East African Integrity and Anticorruption Bill promotes integrity and provides a framework to prevent and combat corruption in the EAC.
Consumer protection		
EAC Competition Act	2006, amended in 2010	The EAC Competition Act aims to promote fair competition in the EAC and in Part VIII to protect consumer welfare.

Sources: OECD's compilation based on relevant EAC policy frameworks.

Regarding human rights, there have been attempts to develop a human rights bill at the EAC level. The East African Legislative Assembly passed the EAC Human Rights Bill in 2012, which still requires the EAC Heads of States' assent to become law (DIHR, 2021[39]). Some thematic EAC policies also refer to specific human and labour rights. One example is the 2018 EAC Gender Policy, which promotes gender equality and refers to equal human and labour rights for men and women in the EAC. This Policy calls on promoting participation of women in leadership and institutionalising gender auditing in both the public and private sectors (EAC, 2018[40]). Another example is the 2016 EAC Child Policy, which aims to promote children's rights in the region by referring to international conventions such as the UN Convention on the Rights of the Child but does not address the prohibition of child labour. The policy calls on the private sector to provide support to realise children's rights, and to adopt national and international child protection policies within their organisations (EAC, 2016[41]).

With respect to the environment, the 2006 EAC Protocol on Environment and Natural Resources Management, the 2010 EAC Transboundary Ecosystems Management Bill, the 2015 EAC Forests Management and Protection Bill, and the 2021 Regional Bioeconomy Strategy address environmental issues and emphasise the role of the private sector and public-private partnerships in the management and protection of natural resources. The 2011 EAC Climate Change Policy also aims to guide Partner States regarding the adoption of measures to address climate change and, among others, seeks to promote the participation of the private sector in its implementation (EAC, 2011[42]).

In relation to anti-corruption, the 2019 East African Integrity and Anticorruption Bill promotes integrity and provides a framework to prevent and combat corruption, but focuses on the public sector and does not address the role of the private sector in combating the phenomenon (EAC, 2021[43]). Moreover, according to an EAC report, the Community is currently developing a Protocol on Preventing and Combatting Corruption (EAC, 2023[44]).

EAC sectoral frameworks provide entry points for RBC

In addition to thematic frameworks addressing aspects covered by the OECD MNE Guidelines, the EAC has formulated sector-specific policies that are relevant for RBC, particularly due to their focus on the extractive and agriculture sectors.

In the mining and extractive sector, these policies are based on overarching policy frameworks, notably the EAC Treaty, the African Mining Vision, and the frameworks of the International Conference on the Great Lakes Region (ICGLR), which all stress the importance of fostering sustainable and responsible mining practices. The 2017 EAC Mining Bill thus seeks to harmonise mining regulations to promote the protection of the environment and human rights in mining practices. It includes provisions on the rights of affected communities, artisanal and small-scale mining, and environmental protection and management (Clause 14 and 15, EAC Mining Bill). More precisely, the Bill refers to the protection of the human rights of local communities, calling on EAC Partner States "to ensure that inhabitants or communities, who have to be resettled as a result of being displaced by a proposed mining operation, are resettled by the holder on suitable alternate land, with due regard to their human rights, economic well-being, customs, traditions, social and cultural values" (Clause 10.6). It also refers to the promotion of sustainable working conditions, stating that "Partner States shall adopt appropriate legislation to provide for artisanal and small-scale mining, which promotes the realization of safe, efficient and environmentally sustainable working conditions for the miners" (Clause 14.1) (EAC, 2017[45]).

For the agricultural sector, the 2006 EAC Agriculture and Rural Development Policy sets out the broad objective to promote sustainable use and management of natural resources (soil, water, fisheries and forest) to conserve the environment (EAC, 2006[46]). Additional specific policies refer to the role of businesses in achieving sustainability goals in the sector and addressing related issues. For instance, the 2013 EAC Regional Strategy and Implementation Plan for Sustainable Aquaculture calls on the private sector to practice responsible aquaculture, apply best management practices, and conform to wetland and watershed conservation standards (EAC, 2013[47]). The EAC Food and Nutrition Security Strategy and Action Plan (2019-2023) also highlights the role of the private sector in contributing to fair relationships between corporate shareholders and smallholders and to inclusive agricultural value chain development (EAC, 2019[48]).

5.2.3. Limited development of specific policies to promote RBC by EAC Partner States

At the national level, some EAC Partner States have developed specific policies to promote responsible business practices, such as National Action Plans on Business and Human Rights. They have also ratified relevant international agreements, developed legal and policy frameworks in the areas covered by the OECD MNE Guidelines, introduced references to OECD RBC and due diligence standards in such frameworks, and signed trade and investment agreements with provisions relevant for RBC. These are all steps towards the creation of enabling environments for RBC, which could be reinforced.

Kenya and Uganda stand out as the first African countries to have published National Action Plans on Business and Human Rights (NAPs),[4] while a process for developing a NAP is currently underway in Tanzania (Table 5.2). In Kenya, the government started to develop a NAP in 2016 and approved it in 2021. The NAP lays out policy priorities on business and human rights, with a focus on five substantive themes: land and natural resources; revenue transparency; environmental protection; labour; and access to remedy. It also contains policy actions for each of the three pillars of the UNGPs; as well as a chapter on implementation and monitoring (Government of Kenya, 2020[49]). While an Implementation Committee for the NAP was formed in 2021, there is limited publicly available information regarding the implementation and monitoring process of the NAP. In Uganda, the NAP was published in 2021 following a process that began in 2016. It involved various government ministries, as well as CSOs, and UN agencies. Eleven consultations were held across Uganda in 2019, gathering input on eight thematic areas, including land rights, the protection of the environment, and labour rights. The NAP aims to co-ordinate efforts across sectors to promote the respect of human rights in business operations. It contains a detailed budget, output indicators, and mechanisms for follow-up, monitoring, and review. A Multi-Sectoral Technical Committee on Business and Human Rights was established to oversee its implementation. Following its adoption, training sessions to disseminate the NAP have been carried out at the local government level by the Initiative for Social and Economic Rights in partnership with the Ministry of Gender, Labour and Social Development (Government of Uganda, 2021[50]). In Tanzania, the government, in its Human Rights Action Plan (2013-2017), directed the Commission for Human Rights and Good Governance to assist in establishing a NAP through the development of a National Baseline Study on Business and Human Rights, which was published in 2017. After further consultations, in March 2023, the Tanzanian government committed to developing the NAP (DIHR, 2023[51]).

Table 5.2. Development of National Action Plans and ratification of key international agreements

	NAP on RBC / BHR	Core UN Conventions on Human Rights	Fundamental ILO Conventions	Kyoto Protocol	Paris Agreement	Convention on Biological Diversity	UN Convention against Corruption
BDI	□	7/9	8/11	■	■	■	■
COD	□	7/9	8/11	■	■	■	■
KEN	■	7/9	7/11	■	■	■	■
RWA	□	8/9	10/11	■	■	■	■
SSD	□	7/9	7/11	□	■	□	■
TZA	◘	6/9	8/11	■	■	■	■
UGA	■	8/9	8/11	■	■	■	■

■ Ratified/ developed

◘ Partially ratified/ under development

□ Not ratified/ not developed

Source: OECD's compilation based on relevant EAC policy frameworks.

Beyond NAPs, EAC Partner States have ratified numerous international instruments in areas covered by the OECD MNE Guidelines, including human rights, labour rights, the environment, and anti-corruption, (Table 5.2). Almost all EAC Partner States have ratified the main international agreements on environmental issues and anti-corruption, such as the Paris Agreement or the UN Convention against Corruption. Nonetheless, several EAC countries have not yet ratified all Core UN Conventions on Human Rights nor all Fundamental ILO Conventions. For instance, most Partner States have not yet ratified the International Convention on the Protection of the Rights of All Migrant Workers and Members of their Families nor the ILO Occupational Safety and Health Convention.

EAC Partner States have also developed national legal frameworks in areas covered by the OECD MNE Guidelines (see Annex C), as well as sector-specific legislation addressing labour and environmental matters in the mining and agricultural sectors. In this context, various EAC governments have sought to include references to OECD RBC and due diligence instruments in their legal and policy frameworks. For example, the DRC and Rwanda have referenced the OECD Minerals Guidance in their frameworks applicable to the mining sector (Government of Rwanda, 2012[52]). The DRC mandated due diligence on the exploitation and trade of tin, tungsten, tantalum, gold, cobalt, copper, and other strategic minerals by integrating the OECD Minerals Guidance into its legal framework through a Ministerial Decree in 2011 (Government of DRC, 2011[53]). The ICGLR, comprising all EAC Partner States except Somalia, endorsed the OECD Minerals Guidance as crosscutting to the Regional Initiative on the Fight against Illegal Exploitation of Natural Resources, and called on companies sourcing minerals from the Great Lakes region to comply with the Guidance (ICGLR, 2010[54]). It also established a regional certification mechanism for minerals that requires traders to conduct due diligence in accordance with the OECD RBC instruments (OECD, 2011[55]). In many countries of the region, investment policies require investors to consider workers' rights and environmental issues, or to conduct environmental impact assessments and protect indigenous communities. For instance, Burundi's Investment Code requires investors to comply with environmental and labour laws and to submit certificates of environmental compliance (UNCTAD, 2021[56]).

EAC Partner States have also started entering into trade and investment agreements or partnerships that contain provisions relevant for RBC. For instance, the African Continental Free Trade Area includes in its 2023 Protocol on Investment an article on Corporate Social Responsibility (CSR) structured in two parts. On the one hand, the clause contains a series of non-binding CSR principles and standards that investors and their investments should strive to respect. On the other, through this clause, States commit to encourage investors operating on their territory or subject to their jurisdiction to integrate in their internal policies internationally recognised CSR principles and standards (Article 38) (WTI, 2023[57]).

Burundi, the DRC, Kenya, Rwanda, Somalia and Uganda are also members of the Common Market for Eastern and Southern Africa (COMESA), which has a Revised Investment Agreement for the COMESA Common Investment Area (CCIA). The CCIA contains a clause titled "business ethics and human rights" (Article 29), which provides that investors and their investments shall observe the UNGPs; support and respect the protection of internationally proclaimed human rights; ensure that they are not complicit in human rights abuses; and eliminate all forms of forced and compulsory labour, among others. The CCIA also contains a clause titled "corporate social responsibility" pursuant to which investors and their investments should *inter alia* act in accordance with fair business, marketing and advertising practices when dealing with consumers and should ensure the safety and quality of goods and services they provide (Article 30) (COMESA, 2018[58]).

Kenya and the EU signed an Economic Partnership Agreement in December 2023, which contains a chapter on trade and sustainable development. The chapter prohibits the lowering of labour and environmental standards to attract trade or investment. It also includes an article on Trade and Responsible Business Conduct and Supply Chain Management in Annex V. This article recognises the importance of RBC practices and calls on promoting RBC and CSR, "including responsible supply chain management, by providing supportive policy frameworks that encourage the uptake of relevant practices by businesses". It also references international standards on RBC and due diligence such as the OECD MNE Guidelines and the OECD Minerals Guidance and seeks to promote "the uptake of such guidance" (Article 11) (EU, 2023[59]).

Recently, several international partnership agreements on the supply of minerals critical to the energy and digital transitions have been signed by EAC countries to attract more investment to these sectors and help enhance value addition, and they also include provisions relevant for RBC, such as cooperation for due diligence and traceability on environmental, social and governance matters.[5]

The awareness and expectations of responsible and sustainable business practices have increased globally and among stakeholders in EAC countries, particularly against the background of human rights, environmental and integrity risks in the agriculture and mining sectors. While the EAC and its Partner States have developed legal and policy frameworks relevant to promote responsible business practices and due diligence, there is still a way to go create an enabling environment for RBC in the region and to improve transparency and the handling of RBC issues in key economic sectors. By making progress in this direction through joint efforts between governments, businesses, and civil society, the EAC region can reinforce its attractiveness for responsible investment and promote sustainable development.

References

Agyemang, et al (2020), *Country-level corporate governance and foreign direct investment in Africa*, https://doi.org/10.1108/CG-07-2018-0259. [16]

BGR (2019), *Mapping of the Artisanal Copper-Cobalt Mining Sector in the Provinces of Haut-Katanga and Lualaba in the Democratic Republic of the Congo*, https://congomines.org/system/attachments/assets/000/001/659/original/BGR_%282019%29_Mapping_of_the_DRC_artisanal_copper-cobalt_sector_engl-min.pdf?1570629800. [9]

COMESA (2018), *Revised Investment Agreement for the COMESA Common Investment Area*, https://www.comesa.int/wp-content/uploads/2020/10/English-Revised-Investment-agreement-for-the-CCIA-28.09.17-FINAL-after-Adoption-for-signing.pdf. [58]

DIHR (2023), *National Action Plans on Business and Human Rights*, https://globalnaps.org/. [51]

DIHR (2021), *Briefing: Opportunities for NHRI Engagement on Business and Huamn Rights at the East African Community*, https://www.humanrights.dk/sites/humanrights.dk/files/media/document/NHRI%20BHR%20Brief_EAC%20Engagement%20Opportunities_2021.pdf. [39]

EAC (2023), *Ethics and Integrity*, https://lms.feaffa.com/wp-content/uploads/2023/02/ETHICS-AND-INTEGRITY-UNIT.pdf. [44]

EAC (2023), *The EAC Quarterly Statistics Bulletin*, https://eac.opendataforafrica.org/ihrbbkg/statistics-bulletin. [61]

EAC (2022), *EAC Trade and Investment Report for 2022*, https://www.eac.int/documents/category/trade-investment-reports. [7]

EAC (2021), *EAC Integrity and Anti Corruption Bill*, https://www.eala.org/documents/view/report-on-eac-integrity-and-anti-corruption-bill2019. [43]

EAC (2021), *Sixth EAC Development Strategy 2021/22 – 2025/26*, http://repository.eac.int/bitstream/handle/11671/24324/6TH%20EAC%20DEVELOPMENT%20STRATEGY%281%29.pdf?sequence=1&isAllowed=y. [6]

EAC (2019), *EAC Food and Nutrition Security Strategy*, https://faolex.fao.org/docs/pdf/mul214502.pdf. [48]

EAC (2018), *EAC Gender Policy*, https://www.jamii.go.tz/uploads/publications/sw1542101555-EAC%20GENDER%20POLICY.pdf. [40]

EAC (2017), *EAC Mining Bill*, http://libraryir.parliament.go.ke/xmlui/bitstream/handle/123456789/4038/EAC%20Mining%20Bill%202017%20Memorandum.pdf?sequence=1&isAllowed=y. [45]

EAC (2016), *EAC Child Policy*, http://repository.eac.int/bitstream/handle/11671/2013/EAC%20Child%20Policy.pdf?sequence=1&isAllowed=y. [41]

EAC (2016), *EAC Model Investment Treaty*, https://edit.wti.org/document/show/pdf/062e9278-4383-4ff9-97b4-a8bbff3eb21c. [37]

EAC (2016), *EAC Vision 2050*, https://www.foreign.go.tz/uploads/eac_vision_2050-_web.pdf. [35]

EAC (2013), *EAC Regional Strategy and Implementation Plan for Sustainable Aquaculture*, https://www.fao.org/3/az018e/az018e.pdf. [47]

EAC (2011), *EAC Climate Change Policy*, https://www.eac.int/environment/climate-change/eac-climate-change-policy-framework. [42]

EAC (2006), *EAC Agricultural and Rural Development Policy (EAC-ARDP)*, https://www.eac.int/agriculture#:~:text=The%20EAC%20Agricultural%20and%20Rural,security%20in%20the%20EAC%20region. [46]

EAC (2006), *EAC Model Investment Code*, https://www.tralac.org/documents/resources/eac/1378-eac-model-investment-code-july-2006/file.html. [36]

EAC (n.d.), *Investment in Mining*, https://www.eac.int/investment/75-sector/investment-promotion-private-sector-development/176-198-40-investment-in-mining. [2]

EAC (n.d.), *Mineral Resources*, https://www.eac.int/environment/terrestrial-ecosystems/mineral-resources. [5]

EAC (n.d.), *Natural Resources*, https://www.eac.int/why-invest-in-eac/natural-resources. [1]

EAC (n.d.), *The Consultative Dialogue Framework*, https://www.eac.int/gender/civil-society/consultative-dialogue-framework. [38]

EATUC (2021), *Enhancing the capacity of EAC trade unions to advocate for trade & investment policies & agreements that deliver decent work & protect workers' rights*, https://eatuc.org/wp-content/uploads/2022/06/EATUC-Advocacy-Strategy-on-Trade-and-Investment.pdf. [32]

EATUC (n.d.), *About Us*, https://eatuc.org/. [31]

EU (2023), *Economic Partnership Agreement between the European Union and the Republic of Kenya*, https://policy.trade.ec.europa.eu/eu-trade-relationships-country-and-region/countries-and-regions/east-african-community-eac/eu-kenya-agreement/text-agreement_en. [59]

FES (2022), *The State of Business and Human Rights in Africa*, https://library.fes.de/pdf-files/bueros/fes-ua/19589-20221107.pdf. [33]

GI-TOC (2023), *Tarnished Hope - Crime and corruption in South Sudan's gold sector*, https://globalinitiative.net/wp-content/uploads/2023/05/Marcena-Hunter-and-Ken-Opala-Tarnished-hope-Crime-and-corruption-in-S-Sudans-gold-sector-GI-TOC-May-2023-.pdf. [13]

GIZ/ FEC (2016), *Guidance on Corporate Social Responsibility*, https://d-nb.info/1185910042/34. [27]

Government of DRC (2011), *MINISTERIAL REGULATIONS No002//2012/MINIRENA OF 28/03/2012 ON THE REGIONAL CERTIFICATION MECHANISM FOR MINERALS*, https://cdn.globalwitness.org/archive/files/library/note_circulaire_oecdguidelines_06092011.pdf. [53]

Government of Kenya (2020), *National Action Plan on Business and Human Rights*, https://statelaw.go.ke/wp-content/uploads/2020/11/NATIONAL-ACTION-PLAN-ON-BUSINESS-AND-HUMAN-RIGHTS-NOV-2020.pdf. [49]

Government of Rwanda (2012), *Report on the Implementation of the OECD Recommendation on Due Diligence Guidance for Responsible Supply Chains of Minerals from Conflict-Affected and High-Risk Areas*, https://www.bgr.bund.de/EN/Themen/Min_rohstoffe/Downloads/Rwanda-Certification-Mechanism.pdf?__blob=publicationFile&v=2. [52]

Government of Uganda (2021), *National Action Plan on Business and Human Rights*, https://www.ohchr.org/sites/default/files/Documents/Issues/Business/NationalPlans/uganda_approved-national-action-plan-on-business-and-human-rights_august-2021.pdf. [50]

ICGLR (2010), *Lusaka Declaration of the ICGLR Special Summit to Fight Illegal Expliatation of Natural Resources in the Great Lakes Region*, https://ungreatlakes.unmissions.org/sites/default/files/icglr_lusaka_declaration_of_the_icglr_special_summit_to_fight_illegal_exploitation_of_natural_resources_in_the_glr.pdf. [54]

IEA (2023), *Sustainable and Responsible Critical Mineral Supply Chains*, https://www.iea.org/reports/sustainable-and-responsible-critical-mineral-supply-chains. [25]

ILO (2019), *Child labour in mining and global supply chains*, https://www.ilo.org/wcmsp5/groups/public/---asia/---ro-bangkok/---ilo-manila/documents/publication/wcms_720743.pdf. [3]

IPS (2020), *Evaluating Due Diligence Programs for Conflict Minerals: A Matched Analysis of 3T Mines in Eastern DRC*, https://ipisresearch.be/wp-content/uploads/2021/03/eval-ddp-20210217.pdf. [17]

LHRC (2022), *Human Rights & Business*, https://humanrights.or.tz/en/post/resources-center/HRBReport21_22. [29]

NEPAD (2023), *TB in the Mining Sector in Southern Africa (TIMS)*, https://www.nepad.org/content/tb-mining-sector-southern-africa-tims. [10]

OEC (2021), *Observatory of Economic Complexity*, https://oec.world/. [60]

OECD (2024), *Review of G7 Government-led Voluntary and Mandatory Due Diligence Measures for Sustainable Agri-food Supply*, OECD Publishing, Paris, https://doi.org/10.1787/f05af4a1-en. [24]

OECD (2023), *Business Handbook on Due Diligence in the Cocoa Sector: Addressing Child Labour and Forced Labour*, OECD Publishing, Paris, https://doi.org/10.1787/79812d6f-en. [21]

OECD (2023), *Handbook on Environmental Due Diligence in Mineral Supply Chains*, OECD Publishing, Paris, https://doi.org/10.1787/cef843bf-en. [20]

OECD (2023), “Recommendation on the Role of Government in Promoting Responsible Business Conduct”, *OECD Legal Instruments*, OECD/LEGAL/0486, OECD, Paris, https://legalinstruments.oecd.org/en/instruments/OECD-LEGAL-0486. [23]

OECD (2019), *Interconnected supply chains: A comprehensive look at due diligence challenges and opportunities sourcing cobalt and copper from the Democratic Republic of the Congo*, OECD, Paris, https://mneguidelines.oecd.org/Interconnected-supply-chains-a-comprehensive-look-at-due-diligence-challenges-and-opportunities-sourcing-cobalt-and-copper-from-the-DRC.pdf. [4]

OECD (2018), *OECD Due Diligence Guidance for Responsible Business Conduct*, OECD, Paris, https://mneguidelines.oecd.org/OECD-Due-Diligence-Guidance-for-Responsible-Business-Conduct.pdf. [19]

OECD (2015), *Mineral Supply Chains and Conflict Links in Eastern Democratic Republic of Congo*, OECD, Paris, https://mneguidelines.oecd.org/Mineral-Supply-Chains-DRC-Due-Diligence-Report.pdf. [28]

OECD (2011), *The Mineral Certification Scheme of the International Conference on the Great Lakes Region*, OECD, Paris, https://www.oecd.org/investment/mne/49111368.pdf. [55]

OECD/FAO (2023), *OECD-FAO Business Handbook on Deforestation and Due Diligence in Agricultural Supply Chains*, OECD Publishing, Paris, https://doi.org/10.1787/c0d4bca7-en. [22]

Punthakey, J. (2020), "Foreign direct investment and trade in agro-food global value chains", *OECD Food, Agriculture and Fisheries Papers*, No. 142, OECD Publishing, Paris, https://doi.org/10.1787/993f0fdc-en. [15]

The Impact Facility (n.d.), *Project Access: Professionalising ASGM in Kenya and Uganda*, https://www.theimpactfacility.com/commodities/gold/professionalising-asgm-in-kenya-and-uganda/. [34]

UCCA (n.d.), "Uganda Consortium on Corporate Accountability (UCCA) website", https://ucca-uganda.org/about/ (accessed on 13 September 2024). [30]

UN et al. (2019), *Responsible business: Key messages from international instruments*, United Nations/OECD/European Union/International Labour Organization, Social Justice Decent Work, https://mneguidelines.oecd.org/Brochure-responsible-business-key-messages-from-international-instruments.pdf. [18]

UNCTAD (2021), *Law No. 1/19 of 17 June 2021 Amending Law No. 1/24 of 10*, https://investmentpolicy.unctad.org/investment-laws/laws/372/burundi-investment-law-2021. [56]

UNGC (2021), *Un Global Compact Africa Strategy 2021-2023*, https://ungc-communications-assets.s3.amazonaws.com/docs/publications/UNGC_Mobilising%20Business%20in%20Africa_2021_2023.pdf. [26]

UNICEF (2023), *Global Databases*, http://data.unicef.org. [8]

UNSC (2023), *Letter dated 15 December 2023 from the Group of Experts on the Democratic Republic of the Congo addressed to the President of the Security Council*, https://documents.un.org/doc/undoc/gen/n23/364/37/pdf/n2336437.pdf?token=MQVv9LJdAJ0gDIDflz&fe=true. [14]

UNSC (2023), *Security Council Calls on Sudan, South Sudan, to Demilitarize Abyei, Highlights Impact of Sudan Conflict on Area's Political Process, Humanitarian Needs*, https://press.un.org/en/2023/sc15481.doc.htm. [11]

UNSC (2020), *Letter dated 2 June 2020 from the Group of Experts on the Democratic Republic of the Congo addressed to the President of the Security Council*, https://documents.un.org/doc/undoc/gen/n20/114/17/pdf/n2011417.pdf?token=9byyFTK04TpXWthael&fe=true. [12]

WTI (2023), *AFCFTA Protocol on Investment*, https://edit.wti.org/document/show/e5d51824-c467-4e24-922b-3fb376d89550. [57]

Notes

[1] The top items exported in terms of value are precious and semi-precious stones (such as gold) (26%), mineral fuel (mainly crude oil) and petroleum products (18%), coffee and tea (12%), trees and other plants (mainly cut flowers) (3%) (EAC, 2023[61]). In terms of agricultural exports, Kenya, for instance is the third largest exporter of tea and the fourth largest exporter of cut-flowers in the world, while Uganda is among the most important coffee exporters. These statistics do not include the DRC and Somalia, which recently joined the EAC. The DRC's exports are strongly centred on copper and cobalt, with copper accounting for more than 53% and cobalt for more than 26% of its exports in 2021. Somalia exports mostly sheep and goats (42%), and gold (20%) (OEC, 2021[60]).

[2] Definitions derived from ILO (2023), Child Labour Statistics, International Labour Organisation https://ilostat.ilo.org/resources/concepts-and-definitions/description-child-labour-statistics/.

[3] Examples of initiatives include among others the Certified Trading Chains by the German Federal Institute for Geosciences and Natural Resources, the ASM Cobalt Criteria by the Responsible Minerals Initiative, the industry-led International Tin Supply Chain Initiative, Better Mining by the RCS Global Group, the Mutoshi pilot project by Trafigura, and the Just Gold project by IMPACT Africa Canada.

[4] National Action Plans on Responsible Business Conduct or Business and Human Rights represent overarching policy frameworks for government action on RBC formulated through inclusive engagement with stakeholders. So far, NAPs have been adopted by 30 countries worldwide. They serve to outline a shared and evolving national framework for RBC, aimed at preventing and addressing business-related adverse human rights impacts. See DIHR (2023), National Action Plans on Business and Human Rights, https://globalnaps.org/ and OHCHR (2016), Guidance on National Action Plans on Business and Human Rights, https://www.ohchr.org/sites/default/files/Documents/Issues/Business/UNWG_NAPGuidance.pdf.

[5] See, for example, EU-Rwanda Memorandum of Understanding on Sustainable Raw Materials Value Chains (2024), https://ec.europa.eu/commission/presscorner/detail/en/ip_24_822.

Annex A. Discriminatory measures against FDI in EAC Partner States

BURUNDI			
Sector	**Policy Category**	**Comments**	**Legal authority / official source**
0. Horizontal	I. Foreign equity limits (Privatised companies/assets: Between 33% and 50%)	The Committee for the Privatization of Public Enterprises (CIP) can reserve a determined percentage of securities for transfer to Burundian citizens or companies with majority Burundian capital, while setting rules and modalities for subsequent transfers to foreign investors. By the formulation of such provision, it is implied that any such rules would impose discriminatory conditions on subsequent equity sales by the privatised asset owners.	Law Relating to the Organization of the Privatization of Enterprises with Public Participation, Services and Public Works, 2012
	IV. Other restrictions (Government procurement offers preference to locally-owned firms)	Preference is granted to tender submissions from national bidders, defined as companies incorporated under Burundian law or domiciled in member states of regional economic organizations to which Burundi belongs, and owned and controlled in its majority by Burundi nationals and nationals from such states. A foreign bidder may also receive a maximum of 5% price preference if they subcontract at least 30% of the contract's total value to a national company for contracts with decentralized local authorities or their public establishment.	Law No. 1/04 of January 29, 2018 amending Law No. 1/01 of February 4, 2008 on the Public Procurement Code
	IV. Other restrictions (Land/real estate ownership not permitted but leases possible – medium-term: up to 70 years)	Access to land is subject to discriminatory restriction as foreign natural or legal persons (including any legal entity constituted in Burundi whose capital is majority owned by foreigners) are only granted freehold land for specific purposes (industrial, agro-industrial, commercial, social, cultural, scientific or residential use) subject to reciprocity. Otherwise, foreign persons may lease land on a medium-term basis up to 50 years. Foreign natural or legal persons cannot own agricultural land unless under a leasehold term.	Law N°1/13 of August 9, 2011 reviewing the Land Code of Burundi
1. Agriculture	IV. Other restrictions (Land/real estate ownership not permitted but leases possible – medium-term: up to 70 years)	Access to land is subject to discriminatory restriction as foreign natural or legal persons (including any legal entity constituted in Burundi whose capital is majority owned by foreigners) are only granted freehold land for specific purposes (industrial, agro-industrial, commercial, social, cultural, scientific or residential use) subject to reciprocity. Otherwise, foreign persons may lease land on a medium-term basis up to 50 years. Foreign natural or legal persons cannot own agricultural land unless under a leasehold term.	Law N°1/13 of August 9, 2011 reviewing the Land Code of Burundi

	I. Foreign equity limits (Divestment is required: More than 50% up to 67%)	In the mining sector, at least 10% of the shares of a mining company must belong to the government and, in addition, the mining company must ensure the participation of Burundi nationals in the equity capital of the company. As reported by the IFC (2022), the government's practice is to determine in mining conventions that 39% of the capital of the licensed mining company be held by Burundi shareholders, 10% by the government of Burundi and the remaining 51% by the foreign investors (see for instance the Mining Agreement on Rare Earth Deposits Gakara).	Law N°1/21 of October 15, 2013 Providing Burundi Mining Code Decree N°100/193 of June 16, 2015 Providing Mining Regulations of Burundi Mining Agreement on Gakara Rare Earth Deposits
	I. Foreign equity limits (Greenfield and acquisitions: Between 33% and 50%)	For the issuance and renewal of a small-scale mining permit, mining companies with predominantly Burundian shareholders are prioritised. Like for large-scale mining, the state is entitled to a minimum ownership stake (at least 16%) in the operating company's share capital. State ownership is not considered a restriction under the OECD FDIRRI since it applies in a non-discriminatory manner.	Law No. 1/19 of 04 August 2023 amending Law No. 1/21 of 15 October 2013 on the Burundi Mining Code
4. Mining & Quarrying	I. Foreign equity limits (Greenfield and acquisitions: No foreign equity allowed)	Foreign investment in semi-mechanised mining is prohibited.	Law No. 1/19 of 04 August 2023 amending Law No. 1/21 of 15 October 2013 on the Burundi Mining Code
	I. Foreign equity limits (Divestment is required: More than 50% up to 67%)	Mining companies involved in large-scale mining and industrial quarry exploitation are subject to a minimum state participation in the share capital of the company of 16%, increased by 5% at every permit renewal, and the company must ensure the participation of Burundi nationals in the equity capital of the company too. For the purposes of the OECD FDIRRI, it is assumed that the previous government practice to allow foreign shareholders to own up to 51% of the share capital of the company is maintained under the new Mining Code, 2023 (see IFC, 2022; and the example of the Mining Agreement on Rare Earth Deposits Gakara).	Law No. 1/19 of 04 August 2023 amending Law No. 1/21 of 15 October 2013 on the Burundi Mining Code Mining Agreement on the Rare Earth Deposits of Gakar
	I. Foreign equity limits (Greenfield and acquisitions: More than 67%, but below 100%)	For the authorisation of a purchase and export counter/bureau of mineral substances from artisanal and semi-mechanized operations, at least twenty-five percent of the counter's share capital must be held by Burundian shareholders, with exceptions only if no Burundian shareholders are present.	Law No. 1/19 of 04 August 2023 amending Law No. 1/21 of 15 October 2013 on the Burundi Mining Code Decree No. 100/224 of November 23, 2023 relating to the modalities of application of Law No. 1/19 of August 4, 2023 relating to the Mining Code of Burundi in relation to the Artisanal Mine, the Semi-Mechanized Mine, the Artisanal Quarry and the Mechanized Career

	I. Foreign equity limits (Greenfield and acquisitions: No foreign equity allowed)	Foreign investment in companies providing transport and storage of quarry materials is prohibited.	Law No. 1/19 of 04 August 2023 amending Law No. 1/21 of 15 October 2013 on the Burundi Mining Code Decree No. 100/224 of November 23, 2023 relating to the modalities of application of Law No. 1/19 of August 4, 2023 relating to the Mining Code of Burundi in relation to the Artisanal Mine, the Semi-Mechanized Mine, the Artisanal Quarry and the Mechanized Career
18. Financial Services – Banking	IV. Other restrictions (Establishment of branches not allowed/local incorporation required)	Local incorporation is required for carrying out banking activities.	Law No. 1/17 of August 22, 2017 governing Banking Activities
19. Financial Services – Insurance	IV. Other restrictions (Establishment of branches not allowed/local incorporation required)	Local incorporation is required for carrying out insurance activities.	Law No. 1/06 of July 17, 2020 revising Law No. 1/02 of January 7, 2014 on the Insurance Code of Burundi
22. Real Estate Investment	I. Foreign equity limits (Greenfield and acquisitions: Between 33% and 50%)	Access to land is subject to discriminatory restriction as foreign natural or legal persons (including any legal entity constituted in Burundi whose capital is majority owned by foreigners) are only granted freehold land for specific purposes (industrial, agro-industrial, commercial, social, cultural, scientific or residential use) subject to reciprocity. Otherwise, foreign persons may lease land on a medium-term basis up to 50 years. Foreign natural or legal persons cannot own agricultural land unless under a leasehold term.	Law N°1/13 Of August 9, 2011 reviewing the Land Code of Burundi

DEMOCRATIC REPUBLIC OF THE CONGO

Sector	Policy Category	Comments	Legal authority / official source
0. Horizontal	III. Restrictions on key foreign personnel (Foreign key personnel (i.e. top-level executive positions) not permitted)	Foreigners cannot hold various top-level corporate positions across industries.	Departmental Ordinance 86/001 determining the List of Jobs Prohibited to Foreigners. (JOZ, No. 7, April 1, 1987, p.36) [google translation]
	IV. Other restrictions (Discriminatory local content requirement)	Foreign investors are required to engage Congolese-owned sub-contractors unless exceptionally when local expertise is unavailable or inaccessible and subject to government approval.	Law N° 17/001 of February 08, 2017 Fixing the Rules Applicable to Subcontracting in the Private Sector [google translation]
	IV. Other restrictions (Public procurement legislation provides for a preferential treatment for majority Congolese-owned small and medium-sized enterprises.)	Public procurement legislation provides for a preferential treatment for majority Congolese-owned small and medium-sized enterprises.	Law No. 10/010 of April 27, 2010 on Public Procurement, Art. 37 [google translation]

1. Agriculture	I. Foreign equity limits (Foreign shareholding in enterprises holding a concession to exploit agricultural land is limited to 49%)	Foreign shareholding in enterprises holding a concession to exploit agricultural land is limited to 49%.	Law No. 11/022 of December 24, 2011 on Fundamental Principles relating to Agriculture [google translation]
2. Forestry and Logging	I. Foreign equity limits (Greenfield and acquisitions: Between 33% and 50%)	Medium-sized artisanal forestry activities (i.e. up to 500 hectares) are reserved to majority-owned Congolese enterprises.	Ministerial Order 84/CAB/MIN/ECN-DD/CJ/00 /RBM/2016 of October 29, 2016 on the Conditions and Rules for the Exploitation of Timber [google translation]
4. Mining & Quarrying	I. Foreign equity limits (Greenfield and acquisitions: More than 67%, but below 100%)	Foreign investment in mining and small-scale mining activities is subject to joint-venture requirements with Congolese investors.	Law N° 007/2002 of July 11, 2002 on the Mining Code, as amended [google translation] Loi n°18/001 du 09 mars 2018 modifiant et complétant la Loi n° 007/2002 du 11 juillet 2002 portant Code Minier [google translation]
6. Manufacturing – Chemical, Rubber, Plastics, Fuel Products and Other Non-Metallic Mineral Products	I. Foreign equity limits (Greenfield and acquisitions: More than 67%, but below 100%)	Foreign investment in wholesale of pharmaceutical products and pharmaceutical manufacturing laboratories requires an association with a Congolese pharmacist.	Ministerial Order No. 1250/CAB/MIN/SP/010/CPH/OMP/2015 of September 28, 2015 amending and supplementing Ministerial Order No. 1250/CAB/MIN/S/AJ/01 of March 14, 2000 on the Conditions for Granting Authorizations to Open and Operate Pharmaceutical Establishments [google translation]
12. Distribution – Retail	I. Foreign equity limits (Greenfield and acquisitions: No foreign equity allowed)	Foreign investment in retail of pharmaceutical products is reserved to Congolese pharmacists.	Ministerial Order No. 1250/CAB/MIN/SP/010/CPH/OMP/2015 of September 28, 2015 amending and supplementing Ministerial Order No. 1250/CAB/MIN/S/AJ/01 of March 14, 2000 on the Conditions for Granting Authorizations to Open and Operate Pharmaceutical Establishments [google translation]
	II. Screening and approval (Screening policy mandates consideration of economic interests)	Foreign investment in retail trade is subject to express authorisation by the President of the Republic, except for in the following domains where it has been authorised by decree: gas stations; supermarkets, beverages, electro domestic appliances, luxury clothing and new vehicle dealerships.	Law No. 73/009 of January 5, 1973 amended by Law No. 74-014 of July 10, 1974 on Trade [google translation] DECREE No. 011/37 Laying Down Precautionary Measures for the Exercise of Small Businesses and Retail Businesses [google translation]
13. Distribution – Wholesale	I. Foreign equity limits (Greenfield and acquisitions: More than 67%, but below 100%)	Foreign investment in wholesale of pharmaceutical products and pharmaceutical manufacturing laboratories requires an association with a Congolese pharmacist.	Ministerial Order No. 1250/CAB/MIN/SP/010/CPH/OMP/2015 of September 28, 2015 amending and supplementing Ministerial Order No. 1250/CAB/MIN/S/AJ/01 of March 14, 2000 on the Conditions for Granting Authorizations to Open and Operate Pharmaceutical Establishments [google translation]
	II. Screening and approval (Screening policy mandates consideration of economic interests)	Foreign investment in wholesale trade is subject to an express authorization of the President of the Republic.	Law No. 73/009 of January 5, 1973 amended by Law No. 74-014 of July 10, 1974 on Trade [google translation] DECREE No. 011/37 Laying Down Precautionary Measures for the Exercise of Small Businesses and Retail Businesses

			[google translation]
14. Transport	I. Foreign equity limits (Greenfield and acquisitions: Between 33% and 50%)	Maritime transport, unless as provided for under international maritime agreements, is reserved to vessels flying the national flag, which is granted to vessels in which foreign interests are not greater than 40%.	Ordinance-Law No. 66-98 – Maritime Navigation Code [google translate]
	I. Foreign equity limits (Greenfield and acquisitions: Between 33% and 50%)	Foreign shareholding in radio and TV broadcasting companies is limited to 49%.	Act N°96- 002 of June 22, 1996 Fixing the Terms and Conditions for the Exercise of Press Freedom [google translation]
	IV. Other restrictions (Reciprocity requirement)	Foreign investment in radio and TV broadcasting is subject to a reciprocity condition.	Act N°96- 002 of June 22, 1996 Fixing the Terms and Conditions for the Exercise of Press Freedom [google translation]
16. Media	I. Foreign equity limits (Greenfield and acquisitions: Between 33% and 50%)	Foreign shareholding in printed media companies is limited to 49%.	Act N°96- 002 of June 22, 1996 Fixing the Terms and Conditions for the Exercise of Press Freedom [google translation]
	III. Restrictions on key foreign personnel (Foreign key personnel (i.e. top-level executive positions) not permitted[1])	The director of publications of printed media company needs to be a Congolese national.	Act N°96- 002 of June 22, 1996 Fixing the Terms and Conditions for the Exercise of Press Freedom [google translation]
17. Telecommunications	I. Foreign equity limits (Greenfield and acquisitions: More than 67%, but below 100%)	Foreign shareholding in telecommunication companies is limited to 69%.	Law No. 20/017 of November 25, 2020 relating to Telecommunications and Information and Communication Technologies [google translation]
18. Financial Services – Banking	IV. Other restrictions (Discriminatory local content requirement)	Statutory auditors of banking institutions in the DRC must either be Congolese nationals or legal persons established under the law of the DRC and with capital held in majority by Congolese nationals.	Law N°003/2002 of 02/02/2002 relating to the Activity and Control of Credit Institutions [google translation]
	IV. Other restrictions (Establishment of branches not allowed/local incorporation required)	Local incorporation is required for investing in banking.	Law N°003/2002 of 02/02/2002 relating to the Activity and Control of Credit Institutions [google translation]
19. Financial Services – Insurance	IV. Other restrictions (Establishment of branches not allowed/local incorporation required)	Local incorporation is required for undertaking insurance and reinsurance activities.	Law n°15/005 of March 17, 2015 on the Insurance Code [google translation]
21. Professional Services	IV. Other restrictions (Reciprocity requirement)	Foreign lawyers may be admitted to practice in DRC subject to a reciprocity condition. Only lawyers can constitute and hold equity interests in law firms and partnerships established in DRC.	Ordinance-Law 79-028 of September 28, 1979 on the Organization of the Bar, the Body of Judicial Defenders and the Body of State Agents [google translation]
	IV. Other restrictions (Reciprocity requirement)	Foreign participation in auditing and accounting firms in DRC is subject to a reciprocity condition.	Law N° 15/002 of February 12, 2015 on the Creation and Organization of the National Order of Experts-Comptables [google translation]
	IV. Other restrictions (Reciprocity requirement)	Foreign engineers can be admitted to the National Order of Engineers subject to a reciprocity requirement.	Law N° 18/033 of December 13, 2018 on the Creation, Organization and Operation of the National Order of Civil Engineers [google translation]

	IV. Other restrictions (Reciprocity requirement)	Architectural firms can only be formed by architects members of the National Order of Architects. Foreign architects can be admitted to the Order subject to a reciprocity condition.	Law No. 18/034 on the Creation, Organization and Functioning of the National Order of Architects [google translation]
22. Real Estate Investment	IV. Other restrictions (Reciprocity requirement)	Foreign investment in real estate services (agents and brokers) is subject to reciprocity.	Decree N° 13/032 Of June 25, 2013 Regulating the Practice of the Profession of Real Estate Expert [google translation]
	I. Foreign equity limits (Greenfield and acquisitions: No foreign equity allowed)	Only Congolese nationals are entitled to perpetual land concessions. Legal entities, both foreign and Congolese-owned, are only entitled to limited-term concession modalities, such as land leases up to 25 years, renewable.	Law No. 73-021 Of July 20, 1973 on the General Property Regime, Land and Real Estate Regime and Securities Regime, as amended and supplemented by Law No. 80-008 Of July 18, 1980 [google translation]

KENYA

Sector	Policy Category	Comments	Legal authority / official source
0. Horizontal	IV. Other restrictions (Land/real estate ownership not permitted but leases possible – long-term: over 70 years)	Ownership of land by non-citizens (including a body corporate not wholly owned by one or more citizens) can only be by way of 99-year leases. There is also restriction on ownership of agricultural land by non-citizens (both freehold and leasehold tenure are prohibited).	Constitution of Kenya, 2010 Land Act No. 6 of 2012, as amended Land Control Act No. 34 of 1967, as amended
	IV. Other restrictions (Government procurement offers preference to locally-owned firms)	Public procurement legislation offer preferences for locally-owned companies. The law mandates that, subject to availability and realization of international or local standards, preference must be given to manufactured articles, materials, or supplies wholly or partially mined and produced in Kenya, or assembled in Kenya, with preference also extended to firms where Kenyans hold over fifty-one percent of shares. Such preferences apply for the procurement goods, services and works.	Public Procurement and Asset Disposal Act No 33 of 2015, as amended
1. Agriculture	I. Foreign equity limits (Greenfield and acquisitions: No foreign equity allowed)	Freehold and leasehold ownership of agricultural land by non-citizens (including a body corporate not wholly owned by one or more citizens) is prohibited. For the purposes of the FDIRRI methodology, this is assumed to fully preclude investment by foreign investors in agricultural activities as foreign-owned entities cannot lease or own land for such purposes.	Land Control Act No. 34 of 1967, as amended
4. Mining & Quarrying	I. Foreign equity limits (Divestment is required: More than 67%, but below 100%)	Persons applying for a license relating to small scale mining operations should be a Kenyan citizen or a body corporate where 60% of the shares are held by Kenyan citizens. With respect to large scale mining operations, the licensee is required to list at least 20% of its equity on a local stock exchange within three years after commencement of production.	Mining Act No 12 of 2016
	I. Foreign equity limits (Greenfield and acquisitions: Between 33% and 50%)	Persons applying for a license relating to small scale mining operations should be a Kenyan citizen or a body corporate where 60% of the shares are held by Kenyan citizens. With respect to large scale mining operations, the licensee is required to list at least 20% of its equity on a local stock exchange within three years after commencement of production.	Mining Act No 12 of 2016

	IV. Other restrictions (Discriminatory local content requirement)	The local content requirement mandates that holders of mining licenses prioritize the use of locally made materials and products, employ local services and citizens, and favour companies owned by Kenyan citizens in all mining operations.	Mining Act No 12 of 2016
11. Construction	I. Foreign equity limits (Greenfield and acquisitions: Between 33% and 50%)	A foreign contractor, including a firm incorporated in Kenya in which 51% of the shares are held by a non-Kenyan, is prohibited from undertaking construction works whose value is below limits set in the regulations (works classified as NCA-2 to NCA-8 in the regulation). Foreign contractors may only register and undertake works classified as NCA-1 (whose value is superior to the NCA-2 threshold). In such cases, foreign contractors are required to give an undertaking that it will subcontract or enter into a joint venture with a local person or local firm for not less than thirty percent of the value.	National Construction Authority Act No. 41 of 2011, as amended National Construction Authority Regulations, Legal Notice No. 74 of 2014, as amended
	IV. Other restrictions (Discriminatory local content requirement)	A foreign contractor, including a firm incorporated in Kenya in which 51% of the shares are held by a non-Kenyan, is prohibited from undertaking construction works whose value is below limits set in the regulations (works classified as NCA-2 to NCA-8 in the regulation). Foreign contractors may only register and undertake works classified as NCA-1 (whose value is superior to the NCA-2 threshold). In such cases, foreign contractors are required to give an undertaking that it will subcontract or enter into a joint venture with a local person or local firm for not less than thirty percent of the value.	National Construction Authority Act No. 41 of 2011, as amended National Construction Authority Regulations, Legal Notice No. 74 of 2014, as amended
12. Distribution – Retail	I. Foreign equity limits (Greenfield and acquisitions: Between 33% and 50%)	Individuals or entities cannot engage in mineral dealings without a mineral dealer's licence or permit, which is exclusively available to citizens of Kenya or to corporations where at least sixty percent of the shareholding is held by Kenyan citizens, with limited permissions for holders of specific licences.	Mining Act No 12 of 2016
13. Distribution – Wholesale	I. Foreign equity limits (Greenfield and acquisitions: Between 33% and 50%)	Individuals or entities cannot engage in mineral dealings without a mineral dealer's licence or permit, which is exclusively available to citizens of Kenya or to corporations where at least sixty percent of the shareholding is held by Kenyan citizens, with limited permissions for holders of specific licences.	Mining Act No 12 of 2016
14. Transport	I. Foreign equity limits (Divestment is required: More than 67%, but below 100%)	Companies wishing to be considered for a Postal and Courier Operators license must allot a minimum of 20% of their total shares to individual Kenyan citizens at the end of three years of operation.	Communications Authority of Kenya, Procedure for Licensing Postal/Courier Operators
	I. Foreign equity limits (Greenfield and acquisitions: Between 33% and 50%)	A license can only be granted to a maritime service provider (comprising local shipping lines, port/terminal operators and other auxiliary services) who is a citizen, or in case of a company, where 51% of the share capital is held directly by a Kenyan.	Merchant Shipping Act No 4 of 2009, as amended Merchant Shipping (Maritime Service Providers) Regulations, 2011
	I. Foreign equity limits (Greenfield and acquisitions: Between 33% and 50%)	A foreign equity restriction in the licensing of internal and international air services prohibits the issuance of a license unless the applicant satisfies the Authority that at least fifty-one percent of the voting rights are ultimately held by the State, a citizen of Kenya, or both, and that the aircraft used meets specified registration and operational standards.	Legal Notice No. 167 - The Civil Aviation (Licensing of Air Services) Regulations, 2018

16. Media	I. Foreign equity limits (Greenfield and acquisitions: More than 67%, but below 100%)	Up to 2023, under the National Information Communications and Technology Policy Guidelines, 2020, only companies with at least 30% substantive Kenyan ownership were licensed to provide ICT services, including telecommunications and broadcasting services (up from 20% under the 2006 policy). This equity restriction was lifted by an amendment to the Guidelines, published on 22 August 2023. (For more information, see Bowmans (2023))	Kenya Information and Communications (Broadcasting) Regulations, 2009 National ICT Policy Guidelines 2020
17. Telecommunications	I. Foreign equity limits (Greenfield and acquisitions: More than 67%, but below 100%)	Up to 2023, under the National Information Communications and Technology Policy Guidelines, 2020, only companies with at least 30% substantive Kenyan ownership were licensed to provide ICT services, including telecommunications and broadcasting services (up from 20% under the 2006 policy). This equity restriction was lifted by an amendment to the Guidelines, published on 22 August 2023. (For more information, see Bowmans (2023))	Kenya Information and Communications (Licensing and Quality of Service) Regulations, 2010 Communications Authority of Kenya, "Licensing Procedures", Website Content National ICT Policy Guidelines 2020 Communications Authority of Kenya, Application for an Electronic Communications Service Provider Licence under the Unified Licensing Framework CA/F/LCS/TL 3.7 (February 2021) Communications Authority of Kenya, Application for a Licence as a Telecommunications Contractor, CA/F/LCS/TL 2.5 (February 2021) Communications Authority of Kenya, Application for an Electronic Communications Service Provider Licence under the Unified Licensing Framework CA/F/LCS/TL 3.7 (FEBRUARY 2021) Communications Authority of Kenya, Application for Submarine Cable Landing Rights Licence CA/F/LCS/TL 6.4 (February 2021)
19. Financial Services – Insurance	I. Foreign equity limits (Greenfield and acquisitions: More than 50% up to 67%)	One third of the paid-up capital of an insurer should be owned by citizens of the East African Community Partner States.	Insurance Act No. 1 of 1985, as amended
	I. Foreign equity limits (Greenfield and acquisitions: No foreign equity allowed)	Foreign investment in auxiliary insurance services is prohibited.	Insurance Act No. 1 of 1985, as amended
	III. Restrictions on key foreign personnel (Nationality requirements for board of directors – At least one must be national)	At least one third of the board of directors of an insurance company needs to be formed by citizens of Kenya.	Insurance Act No. 1 of 1985, as amended
	IV. Other restrictions (Establishment of branches not allowed/local incorporation required)	Branches of foreign insurance companies and auxiliary companies are not permitted.	Insurance Act No. 1 of 1985, as amended

Sector	Policy Category	Comments	Legal authority / official source
20. Financial Services – Other Financial Services	I. Foreign equity limits (Greenfield and acquisitions: More than 67%, but below 100%)	At least 15% of the paid up equity share capital of a derivatives exchange shall be held by a Kenyan entity.	The Capital Markets (Derivatives Markets) Regulations, 2016, Part II, Section 17(1)
	IV. Other restrictions (Establishment of branches not allowed/local incorporation required)	Local incorporation is required for carrying out various financial market intermediation activities.	The Capital Markets (Online Foreign Exchange Trading) Regulations, 2017 The Capital Markets (Coffee Exchange) Regulations, 2020 The Capital Markets (Commodity Markets) Regulations, 2020 The Capital Markets (Licensing Requirements) (General) Regulations, 2002, as amended
	IV. Other restrictions (Establishment of branches not allowed/local incorporation required)	Local incorporation is required for engaging in collective investment schemes activities.	Capital Markets Act No. 3 of 2000, as amended Legal Notice No. 173, The Capital Markets (Collective Investment Schemes) Regulations, 2023
	IV. Other restrictions (Establishment of branches not allowed/local incorporation required)	Local incorporation is required for carrying out venture capital activities in Kenya.	The Capital Markets (Registered Venture Capital Companies) Regulations, 2007
21. Professional Services	I. Foreign equity limits (Greenfield and acquisitions: No foreign equity allowed)	Only citizens of Kenya qualify for admission as advocates in the country and to hold ownership in law firms. Foreign advocates may be admitted to practise in Kenya, at the discretion of the Attorney-General, only in specified suit or matter as authorised by the Attorney-General.	Advocates Act No. 18 of 1989, as amended
	I. Foreign equity limits (Greenfield and acquisitions: Between 33% and 50%)	A foreign firm may only be registered as an engineering consulting firm if the firm is incorporated in Kenya and a minimum of 51% of its shares are held by Kenyan citizens.	Engineers Act No. 43 of 2011, as amended
22. Real Estate Investment	I. Foreign equity limits (Greenfield and acquisitions: No foreign equity allowed)	Ownership of land by non-citizens (including a body corporate not wholly owned by one or more citizens) can only be by way of 99-year leases.	Constitution of Kenya, 2010 Land Act No. 6 of 2012, as amended
RWANDA			
Sector	**Policy Category**	**Comments**	**Legal authority / official source**
0. Horizontal	IV. Other restrictions (Land/real estate ownership not permitted but leases possible – long-term: over 70 years)	Foreigners, including a branch of a foreign company, may not own freehold land but may be granted emphyteutic leases and land concessions specifically for investment purposes for 99 and 49 years respectively.	Law N° 27/2021 Governing Land
4. Mining & Quarrying	I. Foreign equity limits (Greenfield and acquisitions: More than 50% up to 67%)	Foreign participation in small-scale mining operations is prohibited. Foreign shareholding in medium-scale mining activities is limited to 60%. No foreign equity restriction applies to large-scale mining activities.	Law N° 58/2018 of 13/08/2018 on Mining and Quarry Operations Regulations of the Chief Executive Officer N° 005/MINES/RMB/2019 of 18/07/2019 Determining Potential Mining Areas, Criteria for Categorisation of Mines, Modalities

			and Requirements for Mineral Licence Application and for Tenders Regulations of the Chief Executive Officer N° 007/MINES/RMB/2019 Of 18/07/2019 Determining Categories of Quarries, Requirements for Acquisition of Quarry Licence and Reporting Annex IV To Regulations of the Chief Executive Officer N° 004/MINES/RMB/2019 of 18/07/2019 Determining the Format and Content of a Mineral Licence and the Content of an Agreement with a Mining or Industrial Quarry Licence Holder - Content of an Agreement for Mineral or Industrial Quarry Exploitation for Medium Scale Mining with a Mining or Industrial Quarry Licence Holder Annex V to Regulations of the Chief Executive Officer N° 004/MINES/RMB/2019 Of 18/07/2019 Determining the Format and Content of a Mineral Licence and the Content of an Agreement with a Mining or Industrial Quarry Licence Holder - Content of an Agreement for Mineral or Industrial Quarry Exploitation License for Small Scale Mining with a Mining or Industrial Quarry Licence Holder
	I. Foreign equity limits (Greenfield and acquisitions: No foreign equity allowed)	Foreign participation in small-scale mining operations is prohibited. Foreign shareholding in medium-scale mining activities is limited to 60%. No foreign equity restriction applies to large-scale mining activities.	Law N° 58/2018 of 13/08/2018 on Mining and Quarry Operations Regulations of the Chief Executive Officer N° 005/MINES/RMB/2019 of 18/07/2019 Determining Potential Mining Areas, Criteria for Categorisation of Mines, Modalities and Requirements for Mineral Licence Application and for Tenders Regulations of the Chief Executive Officer N° 007/MINES/RMB/2019 Of 18/07/2019 Determining Categories of Quarries, Requirements for Acquisition of Quarry Licence and Reporting Annex IV To Regulations of the Chief Executive Officer N° 004/MINES/RMB/2019 of 18/07/2019 Determining the Format and Content of a Mineral Licence and the Content of an Agreement with a Mining or Industrial Quarry Licence Holder - Content of an Agreement for Mineral or Industrial Quarry Exploitation for Medium Scale Mining with a Mining or Industrial Quarry Licence Holder Annex V to Regulations of the Chief Executive Officer N° 004/MINES/RMB/2019 Of 18/07/2019 Determining the Format and Content of a Mineral Licence and the Content of

			an Agreement with a Mining or Industrial Quarry Licence Holder - Content of an Agreement for Mineral or Industrial Quarry Exploitation License for Small Scale Mining with a Mining or Industrial Quarry Licence Holder
14. Transport	I. Foreign equity limits (Greenfield and acquisitions: Between 33% and 50%)	Air transport companies are required to have at least 51% of their voting rights held by citizens or residents of the East African Community for domestic air service licensing, and by citizens and/or residents of Rwanda for international air service licensing, as per the regulations governing aviation services in Rwanda.	Rwanda Civil Aviation Regulations (Part 37: Licensing of Air Services), 2019, as amended
16. Media	IV. Other restrictions (Discriminatory local content requirement)	Until 2021, at least fifty percent of all content provided by radio broadcasters and free-to-air TV licensees must be produced by Rwandan citizens or legal entities majority-owned by Rwandan citizens, with an additional five percent sourced from independent local producers. Since 2022, qualifying conditions for 'local content' are no longer associated with ownership by Rwandan citizens. Hence, these are no longer recorded as restrictions under the OECD FDI RRI.	Regulation Nº017/R/MR-ICT/ RURA/2022 Of 17/01/22 Governing Broadcasting Services in Rwanda Regulations for Broadcasting Services, 2013
	IV. Other restrictions (Discriminatory local content requirement)	Until 2021, at least fifty percent of all content provided by radio broadcasters and free-to-air TV licensees must be produced by Rwandan citizens or legal entities majority-owned by Rwandan citizens, with an additional five percent sourced from independent local producers. Since 2022, qualifying conditions for 'local content' are no longer associated with ownership by Rwandan citizens. Hence, these are no longer recorded as restrictions under the OECD FDI RRI.	Regulation Nº017/R/MR-ICT/ RURA/2022 Of 17/01/22 Governing Broadcasting Services in Rwanda Regulations for Broadcasting Services, 2013
17. Telecommunications	IV. Other restrictions (Discriminatory local content requirement)	Network infrastructure service provider licenses may be granted to any investor, but the licensee must give preference to material and products made in Rwanda and service agencies located in Rwanda and owned by Rwandan citizens, or Rwandan companies that are majority owned by Rwandan citizens.	Regulation No 013/R/EC-ICT/RURA/2021 Of 25/02/2021 Governing Licensing In Electronic Communication
18. Financial Services – Banking	IV. Other restrictions (Establishment of branches not allowed/local incorporation required)	Local incorporation is required for commercial banks and payment services providers.	Regulation 2310-13 of 2018 of the National Bank of Rwanda on Licensing Conditions for Banks Regulation N° 74/2023 of 18/09/2023 Governing Payment Services Providers
	IV. Other restrictions (Establishment of branches not allowed/local incorporation required)	Local incorporation is required for commercial banks and payment services providers.	Regulation 2310-13 of 2018 of the National Bank of Rwanda on Licensing Conditions for Banks Regulation N° 74/2023 of 18/09/2023 Governing Payment Services Providers
19. Financial Services – Insurance	IV. Other restrictions (Establishment of branches not allowed/local incorporation required)	An insurance company and insurance intermediaries must be an entity registered in accordance with Rwandan Laws.	Law 30 of 2021 governing the Organisation of Insurance Business Regulation 2310-14 of 2018 f the National Bank of Rwanda on Licensing Conditions for Insurers and Reinsurers

			Regulation Nº 4230 of 2019 on Licensing Requirements and Other Conditions for Insurance Intermediaries
20. Financial Services – Other Financial Services	IV. Other restrictions (Reciprocity requirement)	Reciprocity is required for foreign investors to obtain authorisation from the central bank (i.e. National Bank of Rwanda) to establish and carry out the activity of securities depositors in Rwanda.	Regulation No 8 of 2010 of the National Bank of Rwanda on the Licensing Requirements Participants in the Central Securities Depository and the Protective Measures of Securities Law 26 of 2010 governing the Holding and Circulation of Securities
21. Professional Services	IV. Other restrictions (Reciprocity requirement)	Access to the legal profession in Rwanda is typically restricted to Rwandan citizens, but qualified lawyers from other countries may be permitted entry if there is reciprocity or under an international convention.	Law No 83 of 2013 establishing the Bar Association in Rwanda and Determining its Organization and Functioning
	IV. Other restrictions (Reciprocity requirement)	Foreign architects and engineers, as well as foreign architecture and engineering firms may obtain authorisation to practice and provide engineering and architectural services in Rwanda subject to reciprocity.	Law No. 26 of 2012 governing the Professions of Architecture and Engineering and Establishing the Institute of Architects and the Institute of Engineers in Rwanda
	IV. Other restrictions (Reciprocity requirement)	Foreign architects and engineers, as well as foreign architecture and engineering firms may obtain authorisation to practice and provide engineering and architectural services in Rwanda subject to reciprocity.	Law No. 26 of 2012 governing the Professions of Architecture and Engineering and Establishing the Institute of Architects and the Institute of Engineers in Rwanda
22. Real Estate Investment	IV. Other restrictions (Establishment of branches not allowed/local incorporation required)	Local incorporation is required for foreign ownership of land not for business purposes.	Law N° 27/2021 governing Land

TANZANIA

Sector	Policy Category	Comments	Legal authority / official source
1. Agriculture	IV. Other restrictions (Discriminatory minimum capital requirement)	Foreign investment in a few coffee-related processing activities is subject to a discriminatory minimum capital requirement.	Tanzania Coffee Industry Regulations, 2013 (G. N. No. 385 of 2013)
	I. Foreign equity limits (Greenfield and acquisitions: Between 33% and 50%)	Foreign shareholding is limited to 49% in the business of selling meat from authorised hunted animals ("game meat").	The Wildlife Conservation (Game Meat Selling) Regulations, 2020
0. Horizontal	IV. Other restrictions (Access to local finance)	Only foreign investors meeting a minimum investment threshold (higher than required from domestic investors) can be entitled to credit from domestic sources. New Investment Act adopted on December 2022 reduced the minimum investment capital for locally owned businesses from USD 100 000 to USD 50 000.	Tanzania Investment Act, 2022, Sections 2 and 31 [google translation] Tanzania Investment Act, 1997
	IV. Other restrictions (Restrictions on (post tax) profit/capital repatriation (e.g. prior approval, quantitative or time limits))	Only foreign investors meeting a minimum investment threshold (higher than required from domestic investors) have access to unconditional after-tax profit and capital repatriation. The new Investment Act adopted on December 2022 reduced the minimum investment capital for locally owned businesses from USD 100 000 to USD 50 000.	Tanzania Investment Act, 2022, Sections 2 and 28 [google translation] Tanzania Investment Act, 1997

	IV. Other restrictions (Restrictions on (post tax) profit/capital repatriation (e.g. prior approval, quantitative or time limits))	Only foreign investors meeting a minimum investment threshold (higher than required from domestic investors) have access to unconditional profit and capital repatriation.	Tanzania Investment Act, 1997
	IV. Other restrictions (Access to local finance)	Only foreign investors meeting a minimum investment threshold (higher than required from domestic investors) can be entitled to credit from domestic sources.	Tanzania Investment Act, 1997
	IV. Other restrictions (Government procurement offers preference)	Government procurement legislation gives preference to firms majority-owned by Tanzanian citizens in respect of contracts for public works and consultancy services, and to joint venture between foreign and local firms for all procurement, including of goods, under international and national competitive tendering.	Public Procurement Act (Chapter 410) of 2011, last amended in 2022
3. Fishing and Aquaculture	I. Foreign equity limits (Greenfield and acquisitions: More than 67%, but below 100%)	Only Tanzanian vessels may be engaged in fishing activities in Tanzania's territorial water and in its Exclusive Economic Zone, unless exceptionally authorised by the Minister; registration of a Tanzanian fishing vessel is reserved to Tanzanian nationals, individuals or corporations owning ships hired out on bareboat charters to nationals of Tanzania, and individuals or corporations in bona fide joint venture shipping enterprise relationships with nationals of Tanzania.	Fisheries Act, 2003 Deep Sea Fisheries Management and Development Act, 2020 Merchant Shipping (Registration of Ships and Licensing of Vessels) Regulations, 2005
	IV. Other restrictions (Access to local finance)	Foreign-owned investors are not entitled to receive investment incentives available to citizen-owned companies conducting fishing activities in the Exclusive Economic Zone.	Deep Sea Fisheries Management and Development Act, 2020
4. Mining & Quarrying	IV. Other restrictions (Discriminatory local content requirement)	Investors in Oil & Gas activities are required to source goods and services from Tanzanian-owned firms.	The Petroleum Act, 2015
	I. Foreign equity limits (Greenfield and acquisitions: No foreign equity allowed)	Foreign investment in companies holding a "primary mining licence" (i.e. small-scale mining) is prohibited.	Mining Act (Chapter 123), 2010, as amended
	I. Foreign equity limits (Greenfield and acquisitions: No foreign equity allowed)	Foreign investment in mining of gemstones is prohibited.	Mining Act (Chapter 123), 2010, as amended
	I. Foreign equity limits (Greenfield and acquisitions: More than 67%, but below 100%)	Foreign investment in mining activities is subject to partnership with indigenous Tanzanian companies.	The Mining (Local Content) Regulations, 2018
	IV. Other restrictions (Discriminatory local content requirement)	Mineral right holders shall give preference to goods and services produced or rendered by Tanzanian citizens and or local companies fully or partly owned by Tanzanian citizens.	Mining Act (Chapter 123), 2010, as amended
6. Manufacturing – Chemical, Rubber, Plastics, Fuel Products and Other	I. Foreign equity limits (Greenfield and acquisitions: More than 67%, but below 100%)	Foreign investment in midstream and downstream Oil & Gas activities is subject to partnership with Tanzanian-owned local companies holding not less than 25% of the interests in the business.	The Petroleum Act, 2015

Non-Metallic Mineral Products			
11. Construction	I. Foreign equity limits (Greenfield and acquisitions: Between 33% and 50%)	Foreign (majority-owned) construction companies can only be temporarily registered for the purpose of carrying out specific construction contracts.	Contractors Registration Act of 1997, as amended Contractors Registration Bylaws, 1999, as amended
12. Distribution – Retail	I. Foreign equity limits (Greenfield and acquisitions: No foreign equity allowed)	Only Tanzanian nationals can own pharmacy retail outlets in rural and peri-urban zones.	Pharmacy (Accredited Drugs Dispensing Outlets) (Standards and Ethics for Dispensation of Medicines) Regulations, 2019
	I. Foreign equity limits (Greenfield and acquisitions: More than 67%, but below 100%)	Foreign investment in dry ports is allowed subject to partnership with Tanzanian nationals holding at least 10% interest in the business.	The Tanzanian Shipping Agencies (Dry Port) Regulations, G. N. No 341 of 2018
	I. Foreign equity limits (Greenfield and acquisitions: More than 67%, but below 100%)	Only Tanzanian ships may be engaged in local trade (passenger and cargo cabotage); registration of a Tanzanian ship is reserved to Tanzanian nationals, individuals or corporations owning ships hired out on bareboat charters to nationals of Tanzania, and individuals or corporations in bona fide joint venture shipping enterprise relationships with nationals of Tanzania.	Merchant Shipping Act, 2003 Merchant Shipping (Registration of Ships and Licensing of Vessels) Regulations, 2005
	I. Foreign equity limits (Greenfield and acquisitions: More than 67%, but below 100%)	Only Tanzanian ships may be engaged in local trade (passenger and cargo cabotage); registration of a Tanzanian ship is reserved to Tanzanian nationals, individuals or corporations owning ships hired out on bareboat charters to nationals of Tanzania, and individuals or corporations in bona fide joint venture shipping enterprise relationships with nationals of Tanzania.	Merchant Shipping Act, 2003 Merchant Shipping (Registration of Ships and Licensing of Vessels) Regulations, 2005
14. Transport	I. Foreign equity limits (Greenfield and acquisitions: Between 33% and 50%)	Foreign shareholding in private shipping agencies is limited to 40%.	Tanzania Shipping Agencies Act 2017
	I. Foreign equity limits (Greenfield and acquisitions: More than 67%, but below 100%)	Foreign investment in port terminal operations and in some miscellaneous port services is allowed subject to partnership with Tanzanian nationals holding at least 10% of the share capital in the port operating company or 25% in the port services company.	Tanzania Shipping Agencies (Port Terminal Operators) Regulations, 2020 Miscellaneous Ports Services Regulations - 2018 GN NO. 343
	I. Foreign equity limits (Greenfield and acquisitions: Between 33% and 50%)	Foreign shareholding in a shipping agent company is limited to 40%.	Tanzania Shipping Agencies (Shipping Agents) Regulations, 2018
	IV. Other restrictions (Discriminatory local content requirement)	The authorised capital required to start a shipping agency business is USD 10 000 for a company wholly owned by a Tanzanian citizen and USD 100 000 for a company owned jointly by a Tanzanian citizen and foreigner. In the case of an inland waterways port, the authorised capital required to start is USD 2000 for a company wholly owned by a Tanzanian citizen and USD 25 000 for a company owned jointly by a Tanzanian citizen and foreigner	Tanzania Shipping Agencies (Shipping Agents) Regulations, 2018
15. Accommodation, Food Services, Arts, Entertainment and Recreation	I. Foreign equity limits (Greenfield and acquisitions: No foreign equity allowed)	Foreign investment in travel agency, tour operators, car rental and mountain climbing and trekking tour operators is prohibited.	The Tourism Act, 2008 Tourism Agents (Registration and Licensing) Regulations, 2015

16. Media	I. Foreign equity limits (Greenfield and acquisitions: Between 33% and 50%)	Foreign shareholding in companies holding a content services licence (i.e. radio and TV broadcasting license) is limited to 49%.	The Electronic and Postal Communications (Licensing) Regulations, 2018, last amended in 2022
	IV. Other restrictions (Discriminatory local content requirement)	Radio and TV broadcasting companies face local content obligations which discriminate against locally established foreign-owned audiovisual producers.	The Electronic and Postal Communications (Radio and Television Broadcasting Content) Regulations, 2018, last amended in 2022
	I. Foreign equity limits (Greenfield and acquisitions: Between 33% and 50%)	Foreign shareholding in printed media companies is limited to 49%, and any change to the shareholding structure of a foreign-owned media company requires the approval of the Director of Information Services Department.	The Media Services Regulations, 2017
	II. Screening and approval[1] (Screening policy mandates consideration of economic interests)	Foreign shareholding in printed media companies is limited to 49%, and any change to the shareholding structure of a foreign-owned media company requires the approval of the Director of Information Services Department.	The Media Services Regulations, 2017
18. Financial Services – Banking	IV. Other restrictions (Establishment of branches not allowed/local incorporation required (financial services and real estate investment only))	Local incorporation is required for undertaking banking activities. Foreign bank branches are not allowed.	The Banking and Financial Institutions (Licensing) Regulations, 2014
19. Financial Services – Insurance	I. Foreign equity limits (Greenfield and acquisitions: More than 50% up to 67%)	Foreign shareholding in insurance companies is limited to 67%	The Insurance Act, 2009
	III. Restrictions on key foreign personnel (Nationality requirements for board of directors – At least one must be national)	At least one third of the members of the board of an insurance company must be citizens of Tanzania.	The Insurance Act, 2009
20. Financial Services – Other Financial Services	IV. Other restrictions (Establishment of branches not allowed/local incorporation required)	Local incorporation required for establishing and managing collective investment schemes in Tanzania.	Capital Markets and Securities Act, Chapter 79 R.E. 2002, as amended
	IV. Other restrictions (Establishment of branches not allowed/local incorporation required)	Local incorporation is required for undertaking financial leasing, microfinance, mortgage financing activities.	The Banking and Financial Institutions (Financial Leasing) Regulations, 2011 The Microfinance (Non-Deposit Taking Microfinance Service Providers) Regulations, 2019 The Banking and Financial Institutions (Mortgage Finance) Regulations, 2015
21. Professional Services	I. Foreign equity limits (Greenfield and acquisitions: Between 33% and 50%)	Foreign shareholding in accounting and auditing firms is limited to 49%.	The Accountants and Auditors (Practising) By-Laws, 2017 The Accountants and Auditors (Registration) By-Laws, 2017, last amended in 2021
	I. Foreign equity limits (Greenfield and acquisitions: Between 33% and 50%)	Foreign participation in engineering companies is limited to minority shareholding.	Engineers Registration Act, 1997, as amended

	I. Foreign equity limits (Greenfield and acquisitions: Between 33% and 50%)	Foreign participation in architectural service companies is limited to minority shareholding.	Architects and Quantity Surveyors (Registration) Act, 2010
22. Real Estate Investment	I. Foreign equity limits (Greenfield and acquisitions: Between 33% and 50%)	Foreign majority investment in land and real estate units are prohibited unless for the purposes of carrying out commercial activities in Tanzania.	Land Act (Chapter 113), 2001
SOUTH SOUDAN			
Sector	**Policy Category**	**Comments**	**Legal authority / official source**
0. Horizontal	I. Foreign equity limits (Greenfield and acquisitions: No foreign equity allowed)	Foreign investors may not own small businesses as these are reserved for South Sudanese nationals only.	Companies Act, 2012
	I. Foreign equity limits (Equity restrictions applies as follows, but foreign investors investment through branches allowed: More than 67%, but below 100%)	Pursuant to the South Sudan Companies Act of 2012, foreign investors are only allowed 69% maximum ownership in all medium and large sized companies. However, foreign companies are allowed to establish a branch in South Sudan which is not subject to local shareholder requirements.	Companies Act, 2012
	IV. Other restrictions (Land/real estate ownership not permitted but leases possible – long-term: over 70 years)	Generally, a foreign investor may not own land, but may lease land for a period of up to 99 years, renewable. However, in the case of agricultural and forestry land, a foreign investor may only lease such lands for up to 30 and 60 years, respectively. These can be renewed upon mutual consent by the parties.	Land Act of 2009, Investment Promotion Act, 2009, Second Schedule, Section 3
	IV. Other restrictions (Government procurement offers preference to locally-owned firms)	A preferential margin of up to 15%, or any other preference, may be accorded to "national providers" (i.e. entities majority owned by South Sudanese persons) or domestically produced suppliers in public procurement proceedings, if authorised or required by regulations enacted under the Public Procurement and Disposal of Assets Act.	Public Procurement and Disposal of Assets Act, 2018
1. Agriculture	IV. Other restrictions (Land/real estate ownership not permitted but leases possible – short-term: less than 30 years)	Generally, a foreign investor may not own land, but may lease land for a period of up to 99 years, renewable. However, in the case of agricultural and forestry land, a foreign investor may only lease such lands for up to 30 and 60 years, respectively. These can be renewed upon mutual consent by the parties.	Land Act of 2009, Investment Promotion Act, 2009, Second Schedule, Section 3
2. Forestry and Logging	IV. Other restrictions (Land/real estate ownership not permitted but leases possible – medium-term: up to 70 years)	Generally, a foreign investor may not own land, but may lease land for a period of up to 99 years, renewable. However, in the case of agricultural and forestry land, a foreign investor may only lease such lands for up to 30 and 60 years, respectively. These can be renewed upon mutual consent by the parties.	Land Act of 2009, Investment Promotion Act, 2009, Second Schedule, Section 3
4. Mining & Quarrying	I. Foreign equity limits (Greenfield and acquisitions: No foreign equity allowed)	Only South Sudanese citizens and companies fully owned by South Sudanese citizens may be granted small-scale and artisanal mining licenses.	Mining Act, 2012

	IV. Other restrictions (Discriminatory local content requirement)	A mining licence title holder shall give employment preference to South Sudanese nationals and preference to competent South Sudanese contractors. The Mining Act does not, however, provide a definition of "South Sudanese contractors". For the purposes of the OECD FDIRRI, this is assumed to be consistent with the concept of 'national provider' enshrined in the Public Procurement and Disposal of Assets Act of 2018, which defines it as "Provider or Contractor registered in South Sudan and owns majority shares by South Sudanese".	Mining Act, 2012
12. Distribution – Retail	II. Screening and approval[1] (Screening policy mandates consideration of economic interests)	The national investor shall be given priority in retail commerce business.	Investment Promotion Act, 2009
14. Transport	II. Screening and approval[1] (Screening policy mandates consideration of economic interests)	The national investor shall be given priority in cars hire and taxi operations.	Investment Promotion Act, 2009
19. Financial Services – Insurance	IV. Other restrictions (Establishment of branches not allowed/local incorporation required (financial services and real estate investment only))	Insurers must be locally incorporated.	Insurance Bill, 2010
21. Professional Services	IV. Other restrictions (Discriminatory local content requirement)	No foreign contractor, institution or firm shall conduct business in South Sudan whether individually or in partnership without engaging the participation of a registered South Sudanese contractor who shall be retained as a senior technical counterpart. Additionally, no contracting firm shall recruit foreign nationals to perform more than 40% of all the professional engineering tasks of the contract project. Moreover, any foreign consultant or consultancy firm wishing to provide engineering consultancy services shall have participation of a person or firm that is duly registered in the national registry.	Engineering Council Act, 2012
	IV. Other restrictions (Discriminatory local content requirement)	No foreign contractor, institution or firm shall conduct business in South Sudan whether individually or in partnership without engaging the participation of a registered South Sudanese contractor who shall be retained as a senior technical counterpart. Additionally, no contracting firm shall recruit foreign nationals to perform more than 40% of all the professional engineering tasks of the contract project. Moreover, any foreign consultant or consultancy firm wishing to provide engineering consultancy services shall have participation of a person or firm that is duly registered in the national registry.	Engineering Council Act, 2012

22. Real Estate Investment	I. Foreign equity limits (Greenfield and acquisitions: Between 33% and 50%)	Generally, a foreign investor may not own land, but may lease land for a period of up to 99 years, renewable.	Land Act of 2009, Investment Promotion Act, 2009, Second Schedule, Section 3
UGANDA			
Sector	**Policy Category**	**Comments**	**Legal authority / official source**
0. Horizontal	IV. Other restrictions (Discriminatory minimum capital requirement)	Foreign Investors require a minimum of USD 250 000 for their investment project to qualify for an Investment License. For domestic investors the minimum requirement is USD 50 000.	Investment Code Act, 2019 Uganda Investment Authority, Checklist of requirements for an investment license, 2019
	IV. Other (Land/real estate ownership not permitted but leases possible – long-term: over 70 years)	Foreign investors (including majority foreign-owned companies established in Uganda) are not entitled to own freehold land in Uganda as domestic investors are, but may lease land for a period of up to 99 years.	Land Act, Cap. 227, 1998, as amended
	IV. Other restrictions (Government procurement offers preference to locally-owned firms)	Government procurement legislation offers preference to majority Ugandan-owned firms in relation to works and services.	Public Procurement and Disposal of Public Assets Act, 2003, as amended
3. Fishing and Aquaculture	I. Foreign equity limits (Government procurement offers preference to locally-owned firms)	Until 2023, only citizens were authorised to carry out fishing activities in Uganda. For the purposes of the OECD FDIRRI, it is assumed, by extension, that only companies owned by Ugandan citizens were eligible for fishing licenses. In 2023, the Fisheries and Aquaculture Act of 2022 entered into force and repealed the previous Fish Act. The new Act does not contain any provision explicitly prohibiting or restricting fishing activities by non-citizens. Hence, assuming no foreign ownership restrictions applies anymore.	Fisheries and Aquaculture Act 2022 Inland Water Transport, 2021 Fish Act, 1970, as amended Business Licences (Miscellaneous Repeals) Act, 2015 Fish (Fishing) Rules, 2010
4. Mining & Quarrying	I. Foreign equity limits (Greenfield and acquisitions: Between 33% and 50%)	Until 2022, small-scale mining activities were reserved to Ugandan citizens and body corporates in which citizens of Uganda held at least 51% of the beneficial ownership of such a body. Since the enter into force of the new Mining and Minerals Act of 2022, artisanal and small-scale mining licences are reserved to Ugandan citizens and companies wholly owned by Ugandan citizens.	Mining and Minerals Act, 2022 Mining Act, 2003
	IV. Other restrictions (Government procurement offers preference to locally-owned firms)	The legislation mandates that every licensee, contractor, and subcontractor prioritize goods and services produced and available in Uganda, requiring a minimum participation of forty-eight percent by Ugandan companies in joint ventures for goods and services not locally available, and allocating at least ten percent of the total evaluation score for national content, emphasizing employment, local goods and services utilization, and technology transfer during bid evaluation	Petroleum (Exploration, Development and Production) Act, 2013
	IV. Other restrictions (Discriminatory local content requirement)	Mining companies are required to give preference to goods produced in Uganda and services provided by Ugandan citizens and/or companies owned by Ugandan citizens.	Mining and Minerals Act, 2022 Mining Act, 2003

12. Distribution – Retail	I. Foreign equity limits (Greenfield and acqu sitions: Between 33% and 50%)	Pursuant to the Trade Licensing Act of 1969, non-citizens (including companies' majority foreign-owned companies established in Uganda) are prohibited from engaging in trading activities outside any city, municipality or town; as well as in specified goods and urban areas which have not been declared a 'general business area'.	Trade (Licensing) Act, 1969, as amended
13. Distribution – Wholesale	I. Foreign equity limits (Greenfield and acquisitions: Between 33% and 50%)	Pursuant to the Trade Licensing Act of 1969, non-citizens (including companies majority foreign-owned companies established in Uganda) are prohibited from engaging in trading activities outside any city, municipality or town; as well as in specified goods and urban areas which have not been declared a 'general business area'.	Trade (Licensing) Act, 1969, as amended
16. Media	IV. Other restrictions (Discriminatory local content requirement)	Local content rules give preference to content produced by Ugandan citizens and companies owned by them.	Uganda Communications (Content) Regulations, 2019
17. Telecommunications	I. Foreign equity limits (Divestment is required: More than 67%, but below 100%)	Telecommunication companies, existing and new, must list 20% of their stake on local securities exchange to renew or obtain a national telecom operator license.	Uganda Communications Act, 2013 Uganda Communications Commission (2023), "Description of Telecom Licenses and Authorisations"
18. Financial Services – Banking	IV. Other restrictions (Establishment of branches not allowed/local incorporat on required)	Local incorporation is required for obtaining a licence to undertake financial institution businesses, which includes the activities of commercial banks, merchant banks, mortgage banks, post office savings banks, credit institutions, building societies, acceptance houses, discount houses, finance houses and any institution which by regulations is classified as a financial institution by the Central Bank.	Financial Institutions Act, 2004, as amended Financial Institutions (Licensing) Regulations, 2005
20. Financial Services – Other Financial Services	IV. Other restrictions (Establishment of branches not allowed/local incorporation required)	Local incorporation is required for obtaining a licence to undertake financial institution businesses, which includes the activities of commercial banks, merchant banks, mortgage banks, post office savings banks, credit institutions, building societies, acceptance houses, discount houses, finance houses and any institution which by regulations is classified as a financial institution by the Central Bank.	Financial Institutions Act, 2004, as amended Financial Institutions (Licensing) Regulations, 2005
21. Professional Services	I. Foreign equity limits (Greenfield and acquisitions: No foreign equity allowed)	Only qualified Ugandan citizens may register, practice and be partners of law firms in the country.	Advocates Act, 1970, as amended
22. Real Estate Investment	I. Foreign equity limits (Greenfield and acquisitions: Between 33% and 50%)	Foreign investors (including majority foreign-owned companies established in Uganda) are not entitled to own freehold land in Uganda as domestic investors are but may lease land for a period of up to 99 years.	Land Act, Cap. 227, 1998, as amended

Annex B. Additional details on classifications

The ITID considers policy area being targeted by evaluating whether a specific design or eligibility condition of the tax incentive relates to one of six policy goals. Column 1 of the below table lists policy areas identified in the ITID. The clusters build on those identified in the OECD FDI Qualities Indicators and the FDI Qualities policy toolkit. The table identifies how economies target these respective clusters, either through eligibility conditions or the design features of tax incentives (columns 2-5).

Table A B.1. Targeting sustainable development through eligibility conditions and design dimensions of investment tax incentives

(1) Sustainable Development Areas	(2) Outcome condition	(3) Sector condition	(4) Preferential treatment for certain qualifying income	(5) Preferential treatment for certain qualifying expenditure
Employment & job creation	(a) Create a minimum number of new jobs;			(a) Wages of newly created jobs; (b) Wages of recent graduates; (c) Wages of employees, including for women or workers with disabilities.
Environmental impact	(a) Ensure some or a certain level of energy efficiency improvement.	(a) Electricity generation from renewable energy sources;[1] (b) Waste management.		(a) Acquisition of machinery for electricity production from renewable energy sources; (b) Improving the energy performance of machinery or buildings (e.g. via building retrofitting).
Job quality and skills	(a) Reach a minimum level of expenditure on training and education; (b) Pay an average wage at a certain level.			(a) Expenditure on training and education of employees; (b) Wages of trainees and apprentices; (c) Training expenditures for women re-entering the workforce or workers with disabilities; (d) Expenditures related to building training facilities.
Local linkages	(a) Source a minimum share of inputs from the local market; (b) Source a minimum share of inputs from local SMEs.			(a) Expenditures on inputs sourced from SMEs.
Promoting Exports	(a) Achieve a minimum export share in sales.		(a) Income from exports; (b) Income from transit trade.	(a) Export promotion expenditure.[2]
Social Inclusion	(a) Employ a minimum share of female workers; (b) Employ a minimum share of workers with disabilities; (c) Founding members of a company must be people with disabilities.			(a) Wages of female workers or workers with disabilities; (b) Training expenditures for women re-entering the workforce or workers with disabilities.

Notes: Eligibility conditions and design features listed in the table are used by at least one economy included in the database. The list may evolve in the future when economy coverage extends.
1. Includes only tax incentives benefiting electricity generation from renewable energy sources, but not electricity generation from non-renewable sources. Tax incentive may be part of a broader special regime that benefits other sector of the economy.
2. Refers to expenses incurred for the purpose of seeking opportunities and promoting the export of goods or services produced in the economy (e.g. publicity and advertisements abroad, export market research, participation in trade fairs amongst others).

Other policy goals commonly targeted with tax incentives relate to infrastructure and innovation. Infrastructure can relate to a broad set of areas, including transport, utilities (e.g. electricity or gas distribution, water and sewage disposal structures), construction or ICT. CIT incentives promoting innovation commonly target R&D-related costs (e.g. wages of R&D employees, current costs of R&D projects, assets) or certain types of income (e.g. income from R&D or registered patents).

Annex C. National frameworks and stakeholders related to RBC

	Government frameworks/policies	Government-led agencies/ initiatives	Business associations/ Workers' Initiatives	Civil Society Organizations
Burundi	**Constitution of the Republic of Burundi 2018:** **Human Rights:** The law the Promotion and the Protection of the Rights of Persons with Disabilities 2018; law on the Prevention and the Protection of the Victims and Repression of Gender Based Violence 2016, Penal Code 2017; the Code of Criminal Procedure 2018 **Environment & Biodiversity:** Art. 35 Natural Resources management, the National Forest Policy of Burundi 2012; and the National Strategy and Action Plan to Combat Soil Degradation 2011-2016 **Climate Change:** National Strategy and Action Plan on Climate Change 2013 **Extractive Sector:** Mining Act 2013 (amended by Law No. 1/19 of August 4, 2023, introducing innovations such as the notion of production sharing Art. 12 Art. **Corruption:** Anti-Bribery Act 2006, Art. 60 of the April 2016 law *"Bearing Measures for the Prevention and Punishment of Corruption and Related Offenses".* **Others:** Burundi Investment Code, enterprises are required to consider environmental issues and employee rights in its investment and business plan. Banking Act in 2017, regulation relating to the protection of consumers of financial products and services.	**Business and Human rights:** Burundi's National Independent Human Rights Commission, the CNIDH, Ombudsman of the Republic of Burundi **Environment:** Geographical Institute of Burundi (IGEBU) and the Burundian Office for the Protection of the Environment (OBPE), 2005 Environmental Impact Assessment and Audit Regulations **Corruption:** Burundi Anti-Corruption Court, Anti-Corruption special squad **Consumers protection:** National Competition Agency (EACA), promotes competition and consumers welfare.	• Burundi Bar Association, implements business human rights initiatives. • Burundian Manufacturers' Association – AIB • Rubeya & Company Advocates provides corporate advisory services, ensuring compliance with legal and regulatory frameworks. • Federal Chamber of Commerce and Industry of Burundi) (CFCIB).	• Consumer associations Burundi (ABUCO) • Association des Employeurs du Burundi (AEB). • Solidarity of the Christian Youth for Peace and Childhood NGO, advocates for the eradication of child labour and trafficking. • CAPAD (Confédération des Associations des Producteurs Agricoles pour le Développement) • promotes producers' rights and advocates for improving the living conditions of farmers.
DRC	**Constitution of the Republic of The Democratic Republic of the Congo 2005:** **Human rights:** Art. 14 Women's Rights Protection and Promotion, Art. 15 Elimination of Sexual Violence, Art. 36 Right to Employment, Art. 38 Freedom of Association, Art. 41 Protection of Minors	**Business and Human rights:** National Human Rights Commission (CNDR), Business Climate Unit 2021, presidential unit to address business climate issues.	• Global Compact Network the DRC. • Federations of Enterprises of the Congo (FEC) • The Federation of Timber Processing Companies (FIB the DRC)	• NGO consortium *"The Congo is Not for Sale"* • Observatory of Public Expenditure (ODEP), raises awareness on the social impact of financial law implementation for transparency and

	Government frameworks/policies	Government-led agencies/ initiatives	Business associations/ Workers' Initiatives	Civil Society Organizations
	Environment & Biodiversity: The Forest Code 2002, the Decree on Hunting, Law No. 14/003 on Protection of Nature, The Environmental Protection Law 2011, 2016 Ministerial Order No. 28/CAB/MIN/ECNDD/23/RBM/2016 sets the conditions for the approval of a consulting firm in environmental and social assessment. The 2023 amendment to Environment Law No. 11/009, aligning country legislation with Paris Climate. **Climate Change:** 2018 Ministerial Order No. 047/CAB/MIN/EDD/AAN/MML/05/2019 setting the approval procedure for REDD+ investments in the Democratic Republic of Congo. **Agriculture:** The National Investment Plan Agriculture (PNIA), aims to reduce poverty and food insecurity by protecting and restoring communal land soils, establishing appropriate institutional and legal frameworks, and revitalizing public-private partnerships in the agricultural sector. **Extractive Sector:** The 2002 Mining Code, 2016 Guidance on Corporate Social Responsibility: Mining Sector in Katanga, 2018 Law No. 18/001 amending the 2002 Mining Code, specifically Article 42: Environmental and Social Instruction. **Labour Standards:** 2009 Child Protection Code on child labour, forced labour, child trafficking, and slavery. **Corruption:** Law 017-2002 of 2002 establishes the Code of Conduct for Public Officials addressing moral integrity, professional ethics, and the fight against corruption. **Others:** the DRC's Public Procurement Act 2010, includes environmental and green growth considerations within its evaluation criteria, Law No. 23/927 on the protection and responsibility of human rights defenders	**Environment:** Congolese Institute for the Conservation of Nature (ICCN), Forest Working Group (GTF) **Extractive sector:** Guide on Corporate Social Responsibility (CSR Guide) for the mining sector, developed by the DRC government, federations of Enterprises of the Congo (FEC), and civil society organizations. **Corruption:** National Agency for the Prevention and Combating of Corruption (APLC).	• Business code of conduct for the private sector in the DRC (BCOC). • COPEMECO (Confédération des Petites et Moyennes Entreprises Congolaises)	accountability. • Pact NGO focuses on reducing child labor, promoting the rights and improving the living conditions of artisanal and small-scale miners. • Action for the Defense of Human Rights (ADDH), local CSO specialised in the extractive sector. • National Coalition against illegal logging (CNCEIB)
Kenya	**Constitution of Kenya 2010:** **Human Rights:** Art. 20 of the Constitution stipulates that the Bill of Rights binds all State organs and persons. The term "persons" includes companies and associations, Art. 22 grants all individuals the right to initiate legal proceedings in court for any denial, violation, infringement, or threat against their rights. Art. 56 addresses the protection of minorities and marginalized groups.	**Business and Human rights:** Kenya Law Reform Commission, Kenya National Commission on Human Rights, Kenya National Human Rights and Equality Commission (KNHREC), National Land Commission NLC and Baseline Assessment on business and human rights in Kenya.	• UN Global Compact Network Kenya • Kenya Association of Manufactures (KAM) • Kenya Private Sector Alliance (KEPSA) • Sustainable Inclusive Business Africa, founded by KEPSA. • Safaricom • Association of Skilled Migrant Agencies of	• Kenya Human Rights Commission (KHRC) • Kenya Land Alliance supports communities to protect their land rights, in a context of oil exploration and drilling. • Hakijamii NGO, promotes social, cultural and

	Government frameworks/policies	Government-led agencies/ initiatives	Business associations/ Workers' Initiatives	Civil Society Organizations
	Environment & Biodiversity: Kenya's National Land Policy 2009, Kenya's Green Economy Strategy and Implementation Plan 2016–2030 (GESIP), The National Wildlife Conservation Strategy, 2030, National Wildlife Policy 2020, and The National Forest Programme (2016–2030). The Environmental Management and Coordination Act, The Water Act, The Companies Act, The Community Land Act, Wildlife Conservation and Management Act, 2013, Forest Conservation and Management Act, Land Act, 2012. **Climate Change:** Wetlands Conservation and Management Policy 2015, The Climate Change Act 13, Kenya National Climate Change Response Strategy. **Extractive Sector:** The Mining Act 2016, The Energy Bill 2015 **Labour Standards:** The Employment Act., Art. 41: Labor Relations, determining the rights of workers, employers, and trade unions, including the right to fair remuneration and reasonable working conditions, Art. 73: Protection from slavery and forced labour, Art. 80: Freedom of association. **Corruption:** The Proceeds of Crime and Anti-Money Laundering Act.10 & 11, The Ethics and Anti-Corruption Commission Act.12. **Others:** 2018 Finance Act, introduces reporting requirements for certain qualifying multinational entities operating in Kenya.	**Environment:** Kenya National Environment Management Authority (NEMA), carries out Environmental Impact Assessments (EIA) and Environmental and Social Impact Assessments (ESIA), Kenya Forest Service (KFS), Kenya Land and Environment Court jurisdiction, Forest Conservation and Management Trust Fund, Forest Investment Facility, National Environment Trust Fund (NETFUND) and Water Service Trust Fund. **Corruption:** Ethics and Anti-Corruption Commission (EACC), National Anti - Corruption Campaign Steering Committee (NACCSC)	Kenya • Law Society of Kenya, delivers BHR trainings.	economic rights of marginalised communities in Kenya. • Haki Madini, coalition of CSOs working in the extractive sector promoting responsible business and protecting local communities. • The Route to Food, coalition of CSOs working in the extractive sector to promote responsible business practices and the proper regulation of pesticides. • Save Lamu, addresses the environmental and social risks associated with the proposed Lamu Port and the Lamu coal power plant. • Centre for Justice and Governance and Environmental Action - (CJGEA) • Kenya Country Guide on Business and Human Rights, developed by the KHRC and the Danish. Institute for Human Rights (DIHR)
Tanzania	**Constitution of the United Republic of Tanzania 1997:** **Human Rights:** Land Acquisition Act 1967, Land Act 1999, Village Land Act 1999, Public Health Act 2009, Persons with Disabilities Act 2010 **Environment & Biodiversity:** Environmental Management Act 2004, The Forest Act 2002, Beekeeping Act 2002 Climate Change: Zanzibar Climate	**Business and Human rights:** Commission for Human Rights and Good Governance (CHRAGG). **Environment:** National Environment Management Council (NEMC), Department of Forestry and Non-Renewable Natural Resources (DFNR), National Environmental Advisory Committee, Chemical Emergency Response Committee, Wildlife Management Area	• East African Crude Oil Pipeline (EACOP). • Tanganyika Law Society, organised workshops to enhance capacity in BHR and raise awareness of human rights and gender dimensions within the extractive sector. • Tanzania Union of Industrial and Commercial Workers (TUICO), advocates for workers' rights and	• Business and Human Rights Tanzania. • Land Rights Research and Resource Institute, (HAKI ARDHI). • Haki Rasilimali Tanzania, advocacy and learning platform focused on the extractive sector. • Business And Human Rights Tanzania (Bhrt), specialist

	Government frameworks/policies	Government-led agencies/ initiatives	Business associations/ Workers' Initiatives	Civil Society Organizations
	Change Strategy 2014 and National Climate Change Response Strategy 2021 Agriculture: 1997 Agricultural and Livestock Policy. **Extractive Sector:** Mining Act (2010 as amended in 2017), 2015 Tanzania Extractive Industries (Transparency and Accountability Act) **Labour Standards:** 2004 Employment and Labour Relations Act, Workers' Compensation Act, 2009 Law of the Child Act on child labor and forced labor **Others:** Tanzania's National Strategy for Growth and Reduction of Poverty I and II (MKUKUTA I and II)	Support Unit, The Southern Agricultural Growth Corridor of Tanzania. SAGCOT. **Corruption:** Prevention and Combating of Corruption Bureau (PCCB), The Ethics Secretariat, Ethics Tribunal, The Zanzibar Anti-corruption and Economic Crimes Authority (ZAECA)	negotiates collective bargaining agreements.	organization working on BHR in Tanzania. • Legal And Human Rights Center (LHRC), first NGO to establish a business and human rights programme. • Haki Madini Tanzania, promotes human rights of miners and mining-affected communities.
Rwanda	**The Constitution of the Republic of Rwanda 2003:** **Human Rights:** Art. 16 Protection from discrimination, Art.19 Child's right to protection, Art. 42 Promotion of human rights, Art. 43. Protection of rights and freedoms **Environment & Biodiversity:** Law Governing Land in Rwanda, Rwanda's National Forest Policy, implemented in 2004 and revised in 2018, National Biodiversity Policy 2011, The Forestry Investment Plan, The National Forestry Research Strategy, The Environment Law 2018, determines the modalities for protecting, conserving and promoting the environment. **Climate Change:** The Environment and Climate Change Law (2019), Rwanda's Green Growth and Climate Resilience Strategy (GGCRS) **Agriculture:** The National Agroforestry Strategy. **Extractive Sector:** Mining Law 2018, Prioritizes education and health in national law and Rwanda's commitment to RBC (with RMB revoking 13 mining licenses due to shortcomings in safety, environmental, and labor standards). **Labour Standards:** Law Regulating Labour 2009, sets the minimum age of employment at 17 for children working in underground mines. Art. 31 Right to form trade unions and employers associations, Art: 32 Right to collective bargaining.	**Business and Human rights:** Rwandan National Commission for Human Rights (NCHR), On 2021 OHCHR-Rwanda and the Ministry of Commerce jointly organised a workshop focused on strengthening the capabilities of stakeholders and practitioners to address human rights violations by multinational corporations (MNCs) and local businesses. **Environment:** Rwanda Environment Management Authority (REMA), Rwanda Green Fund (FONERWA) managed by the government, aims to promote investment in green innovation, Rwanda Development Board (RDB), Center of Excellence in Biodiversity and Natural Resources Management, Rwanda Mines, Petroleum and Gas Board (RMB) **Corruption:** The Rwanda National Public Prosecution Authority, Rwanda National Anticorruption Advisory Council	• Rwanda Mining Association, ensures compliance with relevant directives and legislation among its members through advocacy and capacity building. • The Rwanda Private Sector Federation (RPSF) • Rwanda Association of Manufacturers (RAM)	• Legal Aid Forum Rwanda, a coalition of 40 diverse CSOs providing legal representation to poor and vulnerable individuals and engaging in BHR promotion. • Collectif Des Ligues Et Associations De Défense Des Droits De L'homme Au Rwanda (CLADHO) • Rwanda Initiative for Sustainable Development (RISD) promote, economic empowerment and poverty reduction of vulnerable communities through equitable access and control of land and natural resources towards. • Rwanda Mining Association

	Government frameworks/policies	Government-led agencies/ initiatives	Business associations/ Workers' Initiatives	Civil Society Organizations
	Top of Form **Corruption:** Law on the protection of whistleblowers, Organic Law on Leadership Code of Conduct, Law on prevention, suppression, and punishment of corruption related offenses.			
South Sudan	**The Transitional Constitution of the Republic of South Sudan 2011:** Human Rights: Art.16 Rights of Women (equal pay) Art.20 Right to Litigation, 25. Freedom of Assembly and Association, freedom of association, including the right to form or join associations and trade or professional unions for the protection of his or her interests. **Environment:** 2009 Investment Promotion Act, investors are required to adhere to environmentally friendly rules (ESG) and 2009 Land Act, regulates investment activities on land acquired from local communities. **Extractive Sector:** Petroleum Act 2012 and the Mining Act of 2012, align the country's mining sector with international standards, encompassing licensing, environmental protection measures, the protection of community land rights, and the conduct of Environmental Impact Assessments. **Labour Standards:** Labour Act 2017, establishes a legal framework for the minimum employment conditions, regulates labour relations, and ensures workplace health and safety. **Corruption:** 2009 Southern Sudan Anti-Corruption Commission (SSACC) Act., Anti-Money Laundering and Counter Terrorist Financing Act., 2011, The Public Financial Management and Accountability Act. 2012,	**Corruption:** The National Audit Chamber The Anti-Corruption Commission. Financial Intelligence Unit.	• South Sudan Business Community & Employers Federation • Warrap Worker Union in South Sudan	• The Advocates For Human Rights & Democracy • South Sudan Workers' Trade Union Federation • Youth Alliance Network, • South Sudan Human Rights Defenders Network (SSHRDN)
Uganda	**Constitution of the Republic of Uganda 1995:** **Human rights:** The Persons with Disabilities Act, The Equal Opportunities Act, The Land Act and Land Amendment Act (2004, 2007), The Children Act. **Environment & Biodiversity:** National Environment Act, National Land Policy of 2013, National Land Use Policy 2007, Uganda Strategic Investment Framework for Sustainable Land Management 2010 – 2020, Uganda Forestry Policy 2001,	**Business and Human rights:** The Equal Opportunities Commission, Uganda Human Rights Commission (UHRC), Human Rights and Business Country Guide 2016, developed by the UHRC and Danish. Institute for Human Rights (DIHR), The National Council on Disability, The Industrial Court, The Minimum Wages Advisory B oard, The Tripartite national	• Uganda Manufacturers Association • UN Global Compact Lo cal Network in Uganda • National Conference on ESCR, the UHRC in partnership with universities and CSOs, convened two forums in September 2014 and 2015, aimed at promoting the protection, promotion, and enforcement of economic, social, and	• Advocates Coalition for Development and Environment. • Anti-Corruption Coalition Uganda. • Uganda Coalition for Corporate Accountability. • The United Org. for Batwa Development in Uganda. • The Forest Peoples Programme Supports Indigenous Forest Peoples

	Government frameworks/policies	Government-led agencies/ initiatives	Business associations/ Workers' Initiatives	Civil Society Organizations
	National Wetlands Policy, Fisheries Policy 2003, Uganda Wildlife Policy, National Biodiversity Strategy and Action Plan II (NBSAP II) **Climate Change:** The National Climate Change Policy (NCCP) **Agriculture:** The National Agriculture Policy 2010 **Labour Standards:** The Employment Act.24, The Worker's Compensation Act.25 The Occupational Health & Safety Act, Prevention of Trafficking in Persons Act, 2009, The National Tripartite Charter on Labour Rela tions 2013,Decent Work Country Program me (2013-2017). **Corruption:** The Public Procurement and Disposal of Public Assets Authority Act, Code of Ethical Standards	charter on industrial relations. **Environment:** The Forestry Sector Support Department; the National Forestry Authority; District Forestry Services; Environmental Protection Police Unit, The National Environment Mana gement Authority (NEMA) **Corruption:** The Uganda Legal Information Institute	cultural rights in Uganda, including BHR. • National Union of Plantation and Agricultural Workers. • Private Sector Foundation of Uganda. • Uganda Women Entrepreneurs Association.	protect their land rights and human rights • National Association of Professional Environmentalists • HURINET, network of human rights international and national organisations • Uganda Consortium on Corporate Responsibility • Initiative For Social and Economic Rights. • The Southern and Eastern Africa Trade Information and Negotiation Institute, promotes equitable development through pro-development trade policies in Uganda and East Africa.

www.ingramcontent.com/pod-product-compliance
Lightning Source LLC
Chambersburg PA
CBHW061222240926
51846CB00006B/1319